LEADERSHIP IS
DESTINY

52 LESSONS FROM THE
LIFE OF DAVID
TO AID LEADERS IN
SELF-REFLECTION AND
SELF-AWARENESS

BY
MICHAEL CHUNG

LEADERSHIP IS
DESTINY

52 LESSONS FROM THE
LIFE OF DAVID
TO AID LEADERS IN
SELF-REFLECTION AND
SELF-AWARENESS

by

MICHAEL CHUNG

TEXAS BOOK
PUBLISHERS

Michael Chung
Sugar Land, TX
michaelchung.com

Printed in the United States of America

Paperback $29.85 ISBN: 978-1-946182-11-1
ePub $18.95 ISBN: 978-1-946182-12-8

Published by the
Texas Book Publishers Association
Houston Texas

David replied to the Philistine, "You come to me with sword, spear, and javelin, but I come to you in the name of the Lord of Heaven's Armies—the God of the armies of Israel, whom you have defied."— 1 Samuel 17:45

Contents

INTRODUCTION

Leaders are busy. The responsibilities on their plates are endless. This means time, talent, and energy are limited. Two areas of great necessity for the betterment of the leader are self-reflection and self-awareness, but there is little time to even write in a journal. Sometimes, even during quiet times, there is this slavery to the calendar, which crushes a time to reflect and grow. Even ten minutes can be hard to carve out. This is where help in self-reflection and growth in self-awareness is crucial. Taking a short amount of time each day, five to ten minutes, through the life of David, could be immeasurably helpful in the personal and spiritual growth of the leader.

Leadership is a voyage. The high seas of life possess many dangers that challenge the welfare of the expedition. This book seeks to help leaders improve the destiny of their organizations, navigating the oceans and conquering the sea monsters through the life and wisdom of one of the greatest leaders in history, King David, the second king of Israel.

No one can be a student of the scriptures without significant attention to Israel's second king. David, on the one hand, is a complicated, contorted, and problematic figure; on the other hand, he was one of God's favorites (Psalm 17:8; Acts 13:33). An argument can be made that he was "God's rotten apple." Look at the checklist—murder, adultery, lies, and covetousness—if ever there existed a poster child for breaking the Ten Commandments, David was it. But he was also the prototype of Israel's future Messiah. Jesus will have as one of his titles, the son of David. Yet, when we think of David, he is most known as the apple of God's eye, despite the serious flaws.

Many people, religious or non-religious, are familiar with David, especially the story of Goliath, but David's life is far more profound than this famous story. This book is the first volume of the fruits of the study of a personality that fascinates and rivals the most prominent Biblical figures like Jesus, Moses, Abraham, Peter, John, and Paul.

Having observed sports teams, military, businesses, universities, countries, and churches, one axiom emerges: "Leadership is destiny." The fate of any entity is correlated to its leadership.

Because of the truth of the above axiom, Leaders must get better, but they are busy. This book is structured to offer the maximum teaching and spiritual nourishment on the life of David without spending too much capital. Because leadership is destiny, then an improved leader will increase the positive destination of the organization being lead.

1 Samuel 18:5 (MSG)
Whatever Saul gave David to do, he did it—and did it well. So well that Saul put him in charge of his military operations. Everybody, both the people in general and Saul's servants, approved of and admired David's leadership.

Chosen to be Despised

Leaders will be loathed. To be chosen by God is to be reviled by others.

"Has not the Lord anointed you ruler?
But some . . . despised him and brought him
no gifts."—I Samuel 10: 1, 24, 27

Leadership means being loathed. In theological circles, to be "chosen" suggests words like —"salvation," "predestination," and "sovereignty" —all affirmative expressions. But what about terms like "criticism," "hatred," and "contemptibility?" Do these words ever come to mind? Part of being God's chosen and anointed is to be reviled. Even though the calling comes from the heavens and the anointing from the Almighty Ruler of the universe, being His elect still results in being disliked, just like Jesus was.

Despite having God as their theocratic ruler, Israel wanted a king like the other nations (1 Samuel 8: 4-9). In 1 Samuel 10, God chose Saul as the first king of Israel. If one were to select a king based solely on the "eye test," Saul would be the one. He was the tallest, most handsome man in the land (1 Samuel 9:1-2).

When Samuel anointed Saul king, some did not like him. Even though Saul had not done anything as king, he already had his critics. Being God's chosen does not just mean salvation; it also attracts loathing.

"You will be hated by all for my name's sake.
They will hate you without reason."
Matthew 10:22

There will always be people who hate for no reason other than they hate God or that they are just odious people. Rest assured, the persecuted are in good company. God's chosen will sovereignly suffer the unjust hatred of others.

Prayer Father, help me accept that leadership is synonymous with being loathed. Help me love those who hate me and not let their lack of acceptance impact what you want me to do.

 Discussion Questions

Why do you think some people naturally dislike a leader as they did in Saul's case? Saul had not done anything, yet he was already disliked. _____

_____

Think of someone who did not like you for any reason; why do you think they did not like you? _____

_____

Why is it that some people do not like others for any apparent reason? _____

_____

Was there ever anyone you did not like? Why? Can you pray for them right now? _____

_____

_____

THOUGHTS _____

_____

_____

_____

There Will Be Scoundrels

There are some people who will not like you and others who are just plain rogues. Leaders have enemies just because bad people exist. Don't give them your time and energy.

"But some scoundrels said,
"How can this fellow save us?"
—1 Samuel 10:27

One of the harsh realities of life is that people can be cruel and mean, capable of doing awful things to one another. The pain is compounded when the perpetrator of evil believes they are within religious boundaries that justify their behavior. Countless men and women have suffered under the hands of someone who vindicated their actions as laudatory when, in reality, their acts are straight from the pits of perdition.

Then there are people out there who are just plain reprobates. No matter what you do or how hard you try, they will always be filled with disgust and fury. Great leaders have recognized these types. Instead of wasting capital and energy trying to rehabilitate troublemakers, wise men and women discard or just ignore them, refusing to allow rebels to drain valuable bandwidth that can be used to lead those who are trustworthy. One tenet of life that we must accept: There are people out there who will dislike us just because of who we are. Our very existence breeds dissonance. The reason is beyond understanding. Maybe the way we look, act, or sound sets some of them off. It is what is within a person that makes them feel afraid and vulnerable (Galatians 5:19-21).

Just because someone reacts poorly to your presence does not mean the fault is within you. Many times, it is within the other person who has not humbly dealt with the issues of their heart. They choose to focus on the speck in your eye while ignoring the plank stuck in theirs (Matthew 7:1-5). The Bible is clear: Some people are just plain dogs and pigs (Matthew 7:6). Do not give them your soul. Not everyone will like us, and some people are just plain hateful. These people need to be ignored and not occupy any space in our hearts or minds.

Prayer Lord, help me identify people who are just plain rogues and not allow them to drain my energy form those who deserve my full attention.

 Discussion Questions

Have there ever been people in your life drain you? _____

_____

_____

_____

How can we have healthy boundaries that prevent these people from decreasing our bandwidth? _____

_____

_____

THOUGHTS   _____

_____

_____

_____

_____

_____

Fight or Flight

Leaders face challenges that no one else does. Life will throw significant tests that we do not possess the capacity to overcome. These times either cause us to run and hide due to fear or run to the fight because of faith.

Finally, Saul, the son of Kish, was taken. But when they looked for him, he was not to be found. 22 So they inquired further of the LORD, "Has the man come here yet?" And the LORD said, "Yes, he has hidden himself among the supplies."
—1 Samuel 10:21-22

David said to Goliath, "You come against me with sword and spear and javelin, but I come against you in the name of the LORD Almighty . . . This day the LORD will deliver you into my hands.—1 Samuel 17:45-46

Life inflicts significant trials that elicit great fear. How we face these tests can reveal the condition of our heart; cowardice and courage cannot coexist. Where one resides, the other hides. Cowardice results from leaning too much on our own personal resource in the face of difficult situations. Fear may impede obedience and action.

Courage is an outpouring of a vibrant faith, recognizing that it is not one's own resources that will accomplish the task but God's. David knew this, but Saul did not. When Saul faces the challenge of being the first king of Israel, he hides (1 Samuel 10:21-22). When

David faces Goliath, he sees God's might and runs to the battle (1 Samuel 17:37, 45-47).

Contrasting Saul with David, one quickly understands why David was so close to God's heart while Saul caused God's grief. When Saul was anointed king, God filled Saul with His spirit, in effect, changing Saul spiritually so he could be a good king (1 Samuel 10:9-11). Despite all God did to ensure his success, Saul failed. When faced with the challenge of being anointed as Israel's first king, Saul runs and hides. This fear will plague his entire life.

David, on the other hand, is about 15 years old when confronted by Goliath. Instead of seeing an intimidating giant, David saw an all-powerful God (1 Samuel 17:37). David remembered God's faithfulness to him in the past, which fueled his present life. His confidence that God would deliver him from the nine-foot behemoth was established by God's protection from wild animals (1 Samuel 17:34-36). David saw God and fought while Saul saw himself and fled.

Life is hard. Difficult challenges surround us, and fear is ever trying to dissuade us from entering the battle. We have only two options from which to choose: Focus on ourselves, and run away, or focus on God and run to the fight.

Prayer *Father, there are great challenges that wait for my testing. Help me see your greatness, not my insecurity. May I have the courage to overcome my fears and glorify your name.*

 Discussion Questions

Why do you think Saul hid, but David ran to the challenge? __

_____

_____

Take some time now and think about how God has been faithful to you? How has he provided? Led you? Blessed you? Think about your prayer life? How has he answered your prayers? _____

_____

_____

Were there ever times where you ran from the battle?

_____

_____

What are some of the fears that you were not able to conquer? _____

_____

What are some fears now that could have you running away from the battle? _____

_____

THOUGHTS

_____

_____

_____

_____

Start Well but Finish Better

How a leader finishes speaks to how they lead. Start-ing well is important; finishing well is even more. How you finish reflects how you live.

"The LORD has torn the kingdom out of your hands and given it to one of your neighbors—to David."
1 Samuel 28:17

Saul started off well (1 Samuel 11), but his effectiveness waned in the end. In 1 Samuel 11, Saul saves the city of Jabesh from the Ammonites. This would be the last time the Bible records his success.

After being anointed king, from 1 Samuel 13 on through the end of 1 Samuel 31, Saul's performance deteriorated. He forgot how God filled and used him (1 Samuel 11:6, 13). Saul began fearing people more than God, relying on his own ability (1 Samuel 13:11-13). In the end, Saul committed suicide, and his legacy is one of wasted effort.

Throughout his life, one does not see Saul inquiring of God, leaning on God, or loving God. He becomes very insecure when David led the army to a triumphant victory instead of rejoicing that Israel is safe and secure under his (Saul's) rule. In the end, Saul could not see that success for anyone in the kingdom was a success for himself. Saul's role as king was supposed to bless the nation, not feed his ego.

By all accounts, Saul did not have a bad life. There are no accounts of adultery like David did with Bathsheba. Saul did not murder anyone (although he did attempt to kill David when jealous ego blinded him to God's role in David's success). Thousands were not killed because of his pride, as David did when he took the census (1 Chronicles 21). His children seemed reasonably adjusted, especially Jonathan. Saul had one wife (1 Samuel 14:50) and maybe one concubine (2 Samuel 3:7), while David had at least eight wives and ten concubines.

By all accounts, Saul was much more "evangelical" on paper than David; yet, David is commended as being the apple of God's eye (Psalm 17:8; Acts 13:22). By today's standards, David would be a rotten scoundrel, someone who would be shunned by the evangelical world. But by Biblical accounts, seeing how David started and finished, it is clear that David was close to God's heart (Acts 13:22) while Saul was rejected (1 Samuel 15:26). God knows the heart and, though outside appearances may seem favorable, God sees all. David was close to God while Saul was not. Saul forgot the king who named him king and chose to lean on himself instead of the Lord of the universe.

Leaders must never use their position to fill their egos; instead, they should do everything to uplift the ones they lead.

Prayer   *Lord, help me start and finish well. May I focus on pleasing you, not myself or others.*

 Discussion Questions

Think of someone you know has already retired. How did they finish? _____

_____

What constituted for them a strong or weak finish? _____

_____

_____

What are areas in your life that can prevent you from finishing well? _____

_____

What are some disciplines and accountabilities you can instill to help you not focus on your insecurities? _____

_____

_____

THOUGHTS
_____

_____

_____

_____

_____

_____

The Ministry of Rejection

*When you serve people and give your heart and
life for them, rejection will happen. There are times
when you may not feel appreciated despite hard
work and pure intentions.*

1 Samuel 8:7: "And the LORD told him: "Listen to
all that the people are saying to you; it is not you they
have rejected, but they have rejected me as their king."
1 Samuel 12:2, "I have been your leader from my
youth until this day."

In life, we will experience rejection. Rejection is one of the
most universally painful experiences in life. Leadership can be
downright painful when our best efforts end miserably (1 Samuel
12:1-4). Fortunately, it is not human approval we should desire but
God's. When we have done our best, we never need to fear God's
rejection (1 Samuel 12:5-6).

Samuel is rejected. The people want a king like the nations
around them. It became too hard to follow an invisible God; they
wanted someone they could see. But Samuel can be seen, and he
has poured his heart and soul into the nation, but the people do
not want him anymore. Samuel is dejected, but God assures him
that they did not reject him.

When I hear the word "rejection," my old romantic life comes
to mind. One of my greatest fears during my college years was
dating. I remember the first girl I asked out. I must have dialed

her number more than twenty times before I gathered enough courage to allow the phone to ring without hanging up. Each ring was a ring of terror. I was so relieved when her answering machine picked up. My fear was so great that I asked her out by message on her answering machine (I later heard through a friend that she had accepted my invitation). Since that day, however, I had many prospective dates tell me "no. " These rejections hurt badly, like a knife cutting through my heart. I wanted a wall to form around my heart to prevent future pain.

Rejection hurts. It makes us feel undervalued. It is often a reminder that we have stronger feelings for someone or something than they do for us, creating feelings of inferiority and shame. Rejection is part of life, notably while serving others. Samuel is feeling this rejection. It hurts because he has given so much of himself.

We cannot please everyone and some castoff our most sincere efforts on their behalf. When this happens, we must have the mind of Samuel not to take it personally, knowing that it is God they are rejecting. We must continue to love and fight for the souls of those we serve (1 Samuel 12:23-25). Leadership means rejection, but this should not stop us from serving those God has called us to lead.

Prayer Lord, help me love those who reject me and not allow the fear and sting of rejection to prevent me from doing what you want.

 Discussion Questions

When have you experienced rejection? How did it feel?_____

_____

_____

What do you do to prevent rejection? _____

_____

_____

How can rejection paralyze us from doing what's best?

_____

_____

Why do you feel Israel rejected Samuel and wanted a king?__

_____

_____

THOUGHTS   _____

_____

_____

_____

_____

_____

_____

_____

Lovingly Afflicted

Christian leaders can experience periods where God is forgotten. Oppression is a tool the Lord uses to cause us to remember and call out to Him.

"But they forgot the LORD their God; so he sold them into the hand of Sisera, the commander of the army of Hazor, and into the hands of the Philistines and the king of Moab, who fought against them. 10 They cried out to the LORD and said, 'We have sinned; we have forsaken the LORD and served the Baals and the Ashtoreths. But now deliver us from the hands of our enemies, and we will serve you.' 11 Then the LORD sent Jerub-Baal, Barak, Jephthah and Samuel, and he delivered you from the hands of your enemies all around you, so that you lived in safety.
1 Samuel 12:9-11

Throughout the Old Testament, a pattern existed: God's chosen people forgot Him and lived a life of sin and debauchery, adopting the wicked ways of the pagan nations. Instead of pleasing God, they were worshiping other gods and following other practices. Ultimately, God's people were put into exile, once by Assyria in 722 B.C. Then Babylon captured the southern kingdom of Judah in waves of exile: 605 B.C. (Daniel), 597 B.C. (Ezekiel), 586 B.C., and 581 B.C. (Jeremiah 52:28-30). They forgot all God did for them and built themselves high sacred stones and Asherah poles on every steep hill and under every spreading tree.

2 Kings 7:11-13 reads, "They did wicked things that aroused the Lord's anger. 12 They worshiped idols, though the Lord had said, "You shall not do this." 13 The Lord warned Israel and Judah through all his prophets and seers: "Turn from your evil ways. Observe my commands and decrees, in accordance with the entire Law that I commanded your ancestors to obey and that I delivered to you through my servants the prophets."

God's children did not listen; therefore, they were disciplined.

Many people testify that during a period of rebellion or self-aggrandizement, suffering or affliction brought them back. In times where God is forgotten, He has a powerful way of reminding us He cares.

God brings affliction because He is love. Affliction should be viewed as a gift that our Father in heaven cares deeply about us (Hebrews 12:6). Are you currently suffering? Take heart. It is not because God does not like you; it is because He loves you.

One noteworthy observation, God sends leaders to help deliver Israel out of their distress. Are you a leader God can use that way?

Prayer   *Father, I know you are aware of my propensity to drift away from worshipping you and turning to idols like fortune, wealth, fame, approval, image management, power, control, covetous, and lust, to name a few. Thank you for your grace and love for me that you would bring affliction to wake me up from my sin and move me back to the path of sanctification.*

 Discussion Questions

Think of a time where you suffered. What good did God bring about? _____

_____

_____

What are idols in our life that tempt us? _____

_____

_____

Think of a saint in the Bible or a saint from history that endured suffering. _____

_____

_____

THOUGHTS   _____

_____

_____

_____

_____

_____

_____

Can You Pray for Someone Who Rejected You?

The caring heart and forgiving spirit of a Godly leader empowers him to pray for those who rejected him after moving on to a new place of service.

"23 As for me, far be it from me that I should sin against the Lord by failing to pray for you. And I will teach you the way that is good and right. 24 But be sure to fear the Lord and serve him faithfully with all your heart; consider what great things he has done for you."
1 Samuel 12:23-24

What defines a real leader? There are many litmus tests: teacher, mentor, supporter, vision-caster, servant, and coach. John Maxwell lists 21 indispensable qualities of a leader, including character, charisma, commitment, communication, competence, and courage. However, Maxwell fails to mention one of the most important leadership qualities listed in the Bible: Prayer (especially praying for people you are no longer responsible for).

Samuel was rejected as Israel's leader. His sons, whom he had personally appointed to leadership roles, turned out to be evil and unfit. They were dishonest, perverted justice, and accepted bribes (1 Samuel 8:1-3) – character traits that made them completely inept. As a result, Israel told Samuel they no longer wanted either him or his sons (1 Samuel 8:4-6) leading the nation. Yet his words in 1 Samuel 12:23 are a strong assessment of a caring heart. He told the nation he would continue to pray for them and instruct them in what was right.

One of my mentors pastored in Albuquerque, New Mexico, before relocating to a pastorate in New Jersey. His words uttered years ago, remain seared into my mind. He told me after almost seven years into his service in New Jersey, he still prayed by name every day for every member of his congregation in New Mexico. Another pastoral mentor of mine could recall in detail the current lives of individuals from his former church, years after he left.

The phrase "out of sight; out of mind" is not biblical. The Bible teaches "in my heart; in my prayers." The apostle Paul was especially good about this. Years after he had visited his disciples, he could write with confidence words like:

"I thank my God in all my remembrance of you, 4 always in every prayer of mine for you all making my prayer with joy." (Philippians 1:3-4)

Take time today to pray for as many people as you can, especially those you have served in another community.

Prayer   Lord, I pray you will fill (insert name, names) with joy and peace as they trust in you (adapted from Romans 15:13).

 Discussion Questions

Think about your own prayer life. How much of it is spent praying for the blessing of others? _____

_____

How often do you pray for your family? Pray for them now. __

_____

_____

Friends? Make a list of friends you can pray for here:

_____

_____

Church members? How can we inspire our church to pray for one another? _____

_____

Those who are lost? Think of those you are uncertain of their faith status, begin praying for them to have faith. _____

_____

_____

_____

THOUGHTS _____

_____

_____

_____

Persisting in Sin

Though the act of committing sin is not acceptable,
the act of persisting in it is the
path to destruction.

"Yet if you persist in doing evil, both you and
your king will perish."
1 Samuel 12:25

We make mistakes, but humankind is sinful. If humanity were sinless, Jesus would not have had to die on the cross.

One of the greatest doctrines in the Christian faith is the doctrine of grace, receiving favor that is undeserved, completely one-sided, bathed in the kindness and mercy of God. But grace does not exonerate righteous living and free will to make the right choices. When we persist in sin too long, God may send some type of calamity in hopes of reform (Hebrews 12:6). But if we persist in sin without repentance and change of life, the Bible indicates we will perish.

Great theologians like St. Augustine have stated this axiom: one of God's greatest judgments is to allow someone to remain in sin. The essence of Romans 1:24: rather than sending calamity on those who were living a debauched life, God allowed them to continue in their sin, leaving no hope for repentance and deliverance. Repentance would be impossible in this scenario.

Though grace abounds in the Christian faith and failure is never fatal, continued persistent unrepentant failure is. To continue in sin is the opposite of fearing and serving the Lord with our whole heart. In persisting in sin, we not only dishonor God but also do not appreciate and honor his faithfulness to us in the past (1 Samuel 12:24-25).

Jesus's words in Matthew 5:8 are crucial:

"Blessed are the pure in heart, for they will see God."

Matthew 5:8

In the end, the main reason to stop persisting in sin is to be able to see God. Persistent sin weaponizes depravities like lust, fantasy, jealousy, insecurity, and pride while preventing us from seeing God and experiencing the greatest intimacy known to humankind. One reason David was the apple of God's eye: he did not persist in sin, but once he was aware of his failing God, he repented with great remorse. We all have ambitions and desires in life, if they are competing with our desire to see God, we must fight to mortify them, so they do not cause us to persist in sin.

Prayer *Father, what are the areas I am persisting in sin but not able to overcome? Help me overcome. Lord, do I have blind spots where I am in sin but do not see? Please help me see where I have fallen short and repent.*

 Discussion Questions

Do you have a friend who would be willing to tell you if there are areas of your life where you could be persisting in sin?

_____

_____

Are you willing to ask this friend about your blind spots?

_____

_____

Read Galatians 5:19-21. Which "works of the flesh" stand out?

_____

_____

How can these fleshly works be lessened, and the fruit of the Spirit increase? _____

_____

THOUGHTS _____

_____

_____

_____

_____

Forgetting the Past Fuels Future Failure

Leaders should remember and reflect on God's past faithfulness for present encouragement. Saul started out well, and God filled him with His Spirit; but Saul did not remember God's past faithfulness, leading to his failure as a king.

"But now your kingdom shall not continue. The LORD has sought out a man after his own heart, and the LORD has commanded him to be prince[a over his people, because you have not kept what the LORD commanded you."
1 Samuel 13:14

"The LORD who rescued me from the paw of the lion and the paw of the bear will rescue me from the hand of this Philistine." Saul said to David, "Go, and the LORD be with you."
1 Samuel 17:37

"Those who ignore history are doomed to repeat it," is a famous quote possibly derived from writer and philosopher George Santayana. In its original form, it read: 'those who cannot remember the past are condemned to repeat it.' But the Bible teaches a different message: 'those who ignore the past will be weakened in their present experience of God's power and faithfulness.'

Saul was commanded early to wait seven days for Samuel to come and offer a sacrifice (1 Sam 10:8). But during the battle with

35

the Philistines, he panicked when his followers began to grumble. Saul waited, but could not fulfill the required time, offering the sacrifice after clearly being told to allow Samuel these duties. Samuel states that Saul will not have a legacy; God will seek someone after his own heart (1 Samuel 13:14). Saul forgot God's faithfulness (1 Samuel 11:13) and did not consider the remarkable things God had done for him (1 Samuel 12:24).

Saul started out well. When he was the chosen king, God filled him with His spirit (1 Samuel 10:9-11), being able to rescue the city of Jabesh (1 Samuel 11:1-11), which confirmed Saul's reign (1 Samuel 11:12). But faced with a greater challenge (the Philistines were at war with Saul), the king forgot God's past faithfulness, which leads to his present (1 Samuel 13) and future failure.

Saul knew he had to wait seven days for Samuel to arrive to offer the sacrifice of protection (1 Samuel 10:8; 13:8), but when Samuel did not arrive, and Saul's troops were becoming increasingly concerned; Saul gave in (1 Samuel 13:9-10). As Saul concludes, Samuel arrives and confronts him (1 Samuel 13:10-11). Rather than repenting, Saul made excuses (1 Samuel 13:11-12), blaming his men and Samuel rather than himself. In the past, Saul had been filled by God's spirit and had been able to perform well as king (1 Samuel 11); however, he forgot his anointing and began relying on himself. One reason David was so precious to God was that God's past faithfulness fueled his present faith. When faced with Goliath, David knew God would deliver based on what God had already done for him and who God was (1 Samuel 17:34-37).

Are you in a dire situation right now? Are you tempted to offer the burnt offering before Samuel arrives? Take a step back and remember what God did for you in the past. This will help you lead in the present and future.

 *Lord, is there a situation where I am tempted to act but would benefit from patience? Please show me if I cannot see and help me wait on your timing, not mine.*

 Discussion Questions

What are the areas of my life that are hard to wait for? What are the areas of my life that I want to offer a sacrifice?_____

_____

_____

Are there any current circumstances that you are tempted to move but could benefit from patience? _____

_____

THOUGHTS

Time Does Not Prevent God from Knowing You

Leaders are limited by time, but God is not. Even time cannot prevent Him from knowing and loving you.

"Even before he made the world, God loved us and chose us in Christ to be holy and without fault in his eyes."—Ephesians 1:4

How much does God love you? He has known you even before time (Ephesians 1:4). Saul reigned over Israel for forty to forty-two years. The events of chapter 13, where he disobeys by offering a sacrifice that subsequently led to Samuel pronouncing his rule will end, are likely very early in his reign as king.

Saul began his rule in 1050 BC, and David was born in 1040 BC, so the events in 1 Samuel 13 likely occurred before David was born.

Time is a limiting factor for those who are finite, but it does not limit the infinite God who knew and loved us before time. Even at the beginning of Saul's rule, God knew Saul was not the man. He had chosen David as a successor, even though David had not yet been born (Acts 13:22). This gives us a glimpse into who God is: The God who knows us before time.

Before you were born, God knew you and had plans for your life, equipping you with gifts, talents, personality, and calling. Being faithful to God's word is the only way we can completely fulfill all God has planned for us since the beginning of time. God loves you and has known you intimately since the beginning of time.

Prayer *: you that you are timeless, that you knew me even before I was. You are the great "I am," who has always been. Your existence beyond time is beyond my comprehension.*

Discussion Questions

David was God's choice before he was even born. What does that tell me about God? _____
_____

How does the fact that God knew and loved you before you were even in existence impact how you see God? _____
_____

How does this impact how you see other people? _____
_____

THOUGHTS _____
_____
_____
_____
_____
_____

Ill-Equipped for the Task

*One characteristic of a poor leader is they do not
equip followers to accomplish their assigned duties.
Good leaders equip their followers for the task.*

"So on the day of the battle not a soldier with Saul
and Jonathan had a sword or spear in his hand; only
Saul and his son Jonathan had them."
1 Samuel 13:22

Leadership is destiny. Life's happiness has a correlation with the leadership we are under. I have seen people thrive under excellent leaders and languish under poor leadership.

We must give thoughtful consideration to those we elect to lead, and those we choose to consult before making life decisions. No leader is perfect, but some are decidedly better than others.

Clearly, Scripture does not have a high opinion of Saul's leadership. After Samuel chastised Saul for being unfaithful to the Lord (1 Samuel 13:13-14), Saul continued to rule. Though Saul had been reprimanded, they were still fighting the Philistines. The Philistines sent raiding parties to plunder the land in hopes of destroying the morale of the Israelites.

One thing is painfully clear: Israel was ill-equipped to battle the Philistines, setting the stage for David years down the road. Since there were no blacksmiths in the nation, Israel's army had no swords or spears except for the two owned by Saul and his son Jonathan.

Poor leaders fail to properly equip their followers, making it difficult, if not impossible, for followers to perform the tasks asked of them. Are you in a situation where you are overworked and under equipped? Does leadership ask you to do too much without giving you the resources you need for success? This is a sign you are under a poor leader.

Prayer Lord, help me see the areas where I can grow and help me equip those I lead to be the best at their position.

Discussion Questions

Was there ever a time where someone you were working for did not provide everything you needed to be successful? What could they have done to help you more?_____

_____

_____

What happens if you are in a situation where you want to provide more but do not have the immediate resources? Is there room for creativity and resourcing? _____

_____

_____

An Egocentric Leader is an Unfit Leader

*Leaders who care more about themselves and what
others think will lead their followers into distress.*

"Now the Israelites were in distress that day,
because Saul had bound the people under an oath,
saying, "Cursed be anyone who eats food before
evening comes, before I have avenged myself on my
enemies!" So none of the troops tasted food."
1 Samuel 14:24

Why was David—one who committed murder, adultery, bore
false witness, and was married to multiple women—considered
the apple of God's eye (Psalm 17:8) while someone like Saul, who
was married to one woman, by all accounts did not murder, nor
commit adultery, considered a miserable failure? It appears Saul's
life was about glorifying Saul. Despite the rotten things David did,
his life was about glorifying God.

Notwithstanding Saul's poor leadership in offering the sacrifice
and losing his kingship, God continued to bring the nation victory (1
Samuel 14:20-23). But instead of giving praise to God, Saul foolishly
proclaimed a fast (1 Samuel 14:24). His men were suffering, tired,
and famished. The last thing they needed was to stop eating. A
great leader would have cared for his followers and sought to
refresh and strengthen them, but Saul did not, further placing his
soldiers at risk.

Jonathan, Saul's son, is unaware of his father's decree. When he sees some honey, he eats it, and the Bible says his "eyes brightened (1 Samuel 14:27)." Had Saul been a good leader, it would not have come down to this, but he was not. His son, the one who was next in line to the throne, did not hear Saul's command and ate honey. When Saul heard of Jonathan's disobedience, he wanted his son to die for disobeying his command. That request was the final straw for Saul's soldiers. They fought for Jonathan, pleading to Saul not slay his son.

It should never have come down to this. A poor leader exhausts and burns out his followers, making decisions to cover his own shame and insecurities instead of sacrificing and shepherding on behalf of others. In this case, Israel's soldiers backed Jonathan, and Saul relented from his foolish decree.

Is there a leader at your school, business, or organization who seems bent on burning you out and not seeking to "brighten" your eyes? Chances are, they are not fit to be leading. Great leaders shepherd their sheep; they do not seek to satisfy their insecurities or puff up their egos.

Prayer   *Father, help me leave my ego at the door so I can fully serve those around me.*

Discussion Questions

Was there ever a time where your ego got in the way? What was the outcome?_____

_____

_____

Have you ever worked under someone who made ridiculous commands? How did it influence morale and authority?_____

_____

_____

THOUGHTS

_____

_____

_____

_____

_____

_____

_____

Caving Into Others

Weak leaders cave into the unified opinion of the masses.

But the men said to Saul, "Should Jonathan die – he who has brought about this great deliverance in Israel? Never! As surely as the LORD lives, not a hair of his head will fall to the ground, for he did this today with God's help." So, the men rescued Jonathan, and he was not put to death.
1 Samuel 14:45

There are times when one must stand-alone. The masses will not accept every decision a leader makes. Leadership requires a vision that sees beyond what most people see. Sometimes this foresight leads to a narrow-minded response. Saul was not such a leader. He was myopic, not being able to see beyond himself, making foolish decisions that caused distress.

As mentioned in the last essay, in 1 Samuel 14, Saul decrees: "No one is allowed to eat until Saul has been fully avenged." Jonathan, his son, did not hear the decree and ate honey on the ground. Once Saul was aware of his son's disobedience, he declared his son should be put to death. But his soldiers came to Jonathan's rescue, pleading that Saul spare Jonathan based on his meritorious behavior and stellar contribution to the nation.

Saul relents, overly influenced by the opinions of others to the point that he valued their approval over God's. To be fair, Saul's decision to put Jonathan to death was foolish – he needed to relent of that outlandish decree – but it still highlighted Saul's glowing indwelt insecurity. It was this very characteristic of currying favor to his followers that contributed to Saul's demise. Earlier, it was the crowds' fears and scattering that led Saul to disobey the command and offer the sacrifice before Samuel's arrival (1 Samuel 13:8, 11-12). Here, Saul continues to show he can be swayed by public opinion.

Though leaders do need to compromise and listen to the thoughts of others, there are times when the crowds do not see clearly, but they believe their gaze is 20/20. When a leader caves into narrow-minded opinions, he or she forfeits their God-given divine mantle of leadership. Part of leadership is vision and leading people towards that vision. Often, followers are not able to see what the leader does and rebel as if they see everything. Great leaders do not cave into the demands of the masses when they know a greater future waits.

Prayer *Lord, there are times where I must walk alone in the decision process, help me have the wisdom and understanding to know when to listen to others, and when not to be influenced by the masses.*

 Discussion Questions

Good advice is crucial. Plans succeed with many counselors. But when are the times when the leader must stand-alone?

_____

_____

What are decisions need more input?   _____

_____

_____

What are the areas where the masses will likely not have the right perspective? _____

_____

_____

THOUGHTS

_____

_____

_____

_____

_____

_____

_____

_____

Self-Aggrandized Monuments

Leaders must build up their followers, not shrines to themselves. One sign of insecurity is someone who tries to draw attention to him or herself.

Early in the morning Samuel got up and went to meet Saul, but he was told, "Saul has gone to Carmel. There he has set up a monument in his own honor and has turned and gone on down to Gilgal."
1 Samuel 15:12

One characteristic of grace is the second chance. God is the God of second chances. After utterly failing God in 1 Samuel 13, Saul receives a second chance to redeem his kingship in 1 Samuel 15. The events of 1 Samuel 15 maybe twenty to twenty-five years after the failure in 1 Samuel 13. Enough time has passed for Saul to grow and mature to the point where he can obey.

The command is clear: Wipeout everything in the Amalekite nation (1 Samuel 15:2-3). But just as he did years earlier, Saul failed (1 Samuel 15:7-11), and he knew it or blinded himself from his failure. His behavior shows something was amiss. When Samuel searches to confront Saul, he is told that Saul has gone to Carmel to set up a personal monument to himself (1 Samuel 15:12).

Insecurity, wedded with disobedience, feeds shame's war against the heart and mind, leading to actions of self-glorification. In the story of life, it is easier to corrupt the story in our minds, creating a false narrative, denying the truth rather than facing the reality that we are all broken and hurting, in need of healing that cannot come from our own resources. Saul did not repent and chose to create a story based on lies (1 Samuel 15:13), blaming others (1 Samuel 15:15), and justifying one's actions as worthy (1 Samuel 15:20-21).

Sadly, many of us choose the way of Saul, making personal monuments to ourselves by trying to self-glorify our lives, actions, and accomplishments rather than facing our inner hurts and pains and asking God to change us.

Prayer   *Father, may my life be one that builds models and statues in your honor, not building my own.*

 Discussion Questions

How do we try to build our own statues? _____

_____

_____

Why do we do it? _____

_____

_____

Why do we place our identity in things that are so insecure?

_____

_____

_____

THOUGHTS   _____

_____

_____

_____

_____

_____

Partial Obedience is not Obedience

*Insecure leaders cannot carry out full obedience
because their ego gets in the way. They are unable
to deny personal benefits and unable to deny being
influenced by the opinions of others. Insecure leaders play the "blame game" when they fail, unable to
accept responsibility.*

18 And he sent you on a mission, saying, 'Go
and completely destroy those wicked people, the
Amalekites; wage war against them until you have
wiped them out.' 19 Why did you not obey the LORD?
Why did you pounce on the plunder and do evil
in the eyes of the LORD?" 20 "But I did obey the
LORD," Saul said. "I went on the mission the LORD
assigned me. I completely destroyed the Amalekites
and brought back Agag their king. 21 The soldiers
took sheep and cattle from the plunder, the best of
what was devoted to God, in order to sacrifice them
to the LORD your God at Gilgal."

22 But Samuel replied: "Does the LORD delight in
burnt offerings and sacrifices as much as in obeying
the LORD? To obey is better than sacrifice, and to
heed is better than the fat of rams. 23 For rebellion
is like the sin of divination, and arrogance like the
evil of idolatry. Because you have rejected the word
of the LORD, he has rejected you as king."
1 Samuel 15:18-23

The scene is set. It has been 20 to 25 years after Saul's failure in
1 Samuel 13; God is about to give Saul another chance to redeem

himself. The Amalekites, who a few hundred years earlier attacked Moses, Joshua, and the nation of Israel at Rephidim (Exodus 17:8-14), were going to experience the final judgment of God (Exodus 17:14), who decreed he would blot out the nation of Amalek from under heaven. Saul would be his chosen instrument to finish the job.

Instead of complete eradication, Saul keeps the Amalekite king alive and the best Amalekite cattle, disobeying God's command. Samuel arrives like he did in 1 Samuel 13 and is greeted with a lie that God's orders were carried out. This time, instead of seeing a dead animal sacrificed, Samuel hears live animals bleating (1 Samuel 15:14). Saul must be confronted again for his disobedience. Instead of owning his failure and repenting, Saul plays the blame game, stating that it was his soldiers and not himself who disobeyed (1 Samuel 15:21).

Insecure leaders cannot handle failure, so they often regress into childhood immaturity and try to blame someone else for their shortcomings. Like a child who whines to their parent about their sibling starting an argument or a teenager who spreads a false rumor about a fellow teen whom they detest, insecure leaders play the blame game, not accepting personal responsibility.

When God requests obedience, he demands 100% adherence. Giving a tiny percentage of our income is not a tithe; being kind to some and unkind to others is not loving others. God demands full obedience. Partial obedience is 0% obedience.

Prayer *...ie obey you fully, not partially, but complete 100% devotion. Forgive me when I have failed.*

 Discussion Questions

What are the areas that prevent us from obeying God fully? __
_____
_____

What are some fears you currently have that you are struggling with that could hinder 100% devotion? _____
_____
_____

How is knowing the doctrine of grace helpful when we fail? __
_____
_____

THOUGHTS

_____
_____
_____
_____
_____
_____

The Incommunicable Liar

Christian leaders must understand God possesses attributes beyond our understanding that enable Him to operate outside the natural boundaries we can experience.

"The LORD said to Samuel, "How long will you mourn for Saul, since I have rejected him as king over Israel? Fill your horn with oil and be on your way; I am sending you to Jesse of Bethlehem. I have chosen one of his sons to be king." 2 But Samuel said, "How can I go? If Saul hears about it, he will kill me." The LORD said, "Take a heifer with you and say, 'I have come to sacrifice to the LORD.'"
1 Samuel 16:1-2

One of the modern church's greatest sins is having morphed the image of God to predominantly one of "my friend." Though characteristics of God's love, mercy, grace, and acceptance are vital for followers to understand, so are attributes like his holiness, justice, wrath, and anger. Theological studies break God's makeup into two categories:

(1) His communicable attributes, where the Creator shares in varying degrees with humanity: love, goodness, mercy, and anger; and,

(2) His incommunicable attributes, where He alone possesses the characteristic apart from creation: omnipotence, omniscience, infinity, holiness, immutability, and self-sufficiency.

Sometimes, because of overemphasizing the communicable aspects of God, His unfathomable greatness is misunderstood. God is reduced to fit within a box of our own understanding. However, if we faithfully read the Bible, we can see that God is beyond our realm of comprehension. He is so great that He sometimes uses lies for his glory.

In 1 Samuel 16, God tells Samuel to go anoint the next king of Israel in the house of Jesse. God's choice is made (16:1), but it evokes fear in Samuel, who thinks Saul will kill him. God could have easily told Samuel not to worry, that He would protect him, or God could have sent an angel to strengthen him. Instead, God chose an unconventional avenue for Samuel's protection: A lie.

> "Take a heifer with you and say, 'I have come to sacrifice to the LORD.'3 Invite Jesse to the sacrifice, and I will show you what to do. You are to anoint for me the one I indicate."
> 1 Samuel 16:2-3

God, who is holy and perfect and cannot sin, tells Samuel to lie. Though what Samuel said was not completely false, upon arriving in Bethlehem, he consecrated Jesse and his sons with a sacrifice (16:4-5). That, however, was not his true purpose; and David, the object of his visit, was not even present during the sacrifice.

God is beyond our comprehension. He has the authority to order his servant to lie, and it is not even sin or a violation of His holiness to do so. Part of being a spiritual leader is to worship God, not just in His love and mercy but also in His holiness, justice, and omnipotence. He is beyond our comprehension. Though he gives us His revelation to help us know him, just like Job, when we really understand the grandeur of God, we are less likely to succumb to worshiping our own pride.

 *Father, you are fathomless, your greatness is higher than the heavens are above the earth. Help me know you better.*

Discussion Questions

What are some incommunicable attributes of God that are dearest to you? _____

_____

_____

How can a study of God's attributes help us worship more? __

_____

_____

_____

David could see God's greatness, how can we see God for who he is like David did? _____

_____

_____

Passing the Heart Test

*Leaders must not focus on outward visible charac-
teristics when selecting workers, but understand that
success rests in the inner being of a person.*

7 But the LORD said to Samuel, "Do not consider
his appearance or his height, for I have rejected him.
The LORD does not look at the things people look
at. People look at the outward appearance, but the
LORD looks at the heart."
1 Samuel 16:7

Studies have shown that people who are taller and attractive tend to make more money. Daniel Hamermesh, a professor in economics at the University of Texas, Austin, wrote a book titled Beauty Pays: Why Attractive People Are More Successful. In the book, he argues that nice-looking people earn 3% to 4% more money than someone more average in appearance. Hamermesh estimates that this could end up being up to $230,000 more over, a career. Other studies reveal that taller people tend to earn more than those who are shorter. Clearly, the secular world values the "eye test" when evaluating potential employees.

Saul would have been ideal; he was the tallest and most attractive person in the nation (1 Samuel 9:2), yet, while he is the poster child for passing the eye test, he fails God's test miserably. Passing the eye test does not ensure passing the "heart" test. Too often, power, position, fame, and wealth enamor the human soul. This can lead to incorrect judgment, being overly influenced by outward appearances, leading to a blindness that cannot discern the inner condition. We are so influenced by outward appearances, that the eyes of the heart are unable to see God's leading.

God told Samuel to go and anoint the next king. Upon his arrival at Bethlehem, the elders of the city began to tremble. Samuel assured them his visit was peaceful and then mentioned that he would like to offer a sacrifice. Samuel went to Jesse and consecrated his family in preparation for the anointing. Note that David was not with them. While Samuel is preparing to anoint the next king, the one God chose was herding sheep.

One by one, Jesse's sons appear before the prophet. Samuel is very impressed by the appearance of Eliab, but God was not (16:6-7). After going through seven sons of Jesse, a match was not found. David is an afterthought, not even on his father's radar screen as a potential candidate for the second King of Israel, so he did not even mention that his youngest son was tending the sheep. Samuel, however, asks, and David is summoned. God tells Samuel David is the one.

David was no slouch. He had a fine appearance, too (16:12-13). After being anointed, David is filled with the Holy Spirit just like Saul had been; only this time, David will possess a kingship that will eventually be fulfilled in Jesus (2 Samuel 7:12-16; Luke 1:30-33). God does not look at the outward appearance; he considers the heart. David lived a flawed life but a life that did its best to honor the name of the Lord.

Prayer *Lord, help me not judge people by their outward appearance, help me see their hearts for what it is.*

 Discussion Questions

Why are we so drawn to strong and attractive looking people? _____ _____

Why do we notice things like people's height when we meet them? _____ _____

What are characteristics that constitute a heart like David's? _ _____ _____

THOUGHTS

God's Preparation Method

God will lead you to people and places as preparation for his purposes. David was led to Saul's service about 15 years before he became king (1 Samuel 16:13-23).

So Samuel took the horn of oil and anointed him in the presence of his brothers, and from that day on the Spirit of the LORD came powerfully upon David. Samuel then went to Ramah. 14 Now the Spirit of the LORD had departed from Saul, and an evil spirit from the LORD tormented him. 15 Saul's attendants said to him, "See, an evil spirit from God is tormenting you. 16 Let our lord command his servants here to search for someone who can play the lyre. He will play when the evil spirit from God comes on you, and you will feel better." 17 So Saul said to his attendants, "Find someone who plays well and bring him to me." 18 One of the servants answered, "I have seen a son of Jesse of Bethlehem who knows how to play the lyre. He is a brave man and a warrior. He speaks well and is a fine-looking man. And the LORD is with him." 19 Then Saul sent messengers to Jesse and said, "Send me your son David, who is with the sheep."—1 Samuel 16:13-19

Preparation is one of the most important keys to success. Before God uses you, He prepares you. There are things one can do personally to prepare for a job, but God also has His plan for success. Even before David was born, God knew Saul's line would not reign over His nation, and David would be his choice. After Saul disobeyed God by not destroying the Amalekite nation, God sent Samuel to anoint the next king of Israel in a minimal coronation.

After David's anointing, Saul is besieged by a spirit, leading to emotional distress. David is then found to come and play the lyre. Most likely between the ages of 15 and 20, when David came into Saul's service, he could be around the palace for 10 to 15 years before he would take the throne himself as the second king of Israel, and Israel's standard-bearer as king before Jesus takes the throne (Luke 1:30-33). Before God uses you, He prepares you.

Joseph (see Genesis 37-50) was told early that God had a plan. At age seventeen, he was a captive in Egypt, then spent years suffering in prison; but at the right time, about 13 years after his captivity began, Joseph would become the second most powerful person in the world.

The apostle Paul, converted in Acts 9 when the light of Christ around AD 35 blinded him, did not embark on his first missionary journey until around AD 46. Three of his missionary journeys are recorded in Scripture, but many scholars believe a fourth missionary journey occurred before he died a martyr around AD 68.

God has His preparation process, and it often involves a lengthy period of training before one is ready to don the mantle of his calling. Think about your life as far as you can remember. What brought you extraordinary joy? What things were you naturally good at? Where were you living, and why? What experiences helped shaped you? Where are you living now? What are your gifts, talents, and burdens? What do you naturally gravitate to? These are all parts of God's plan to prepare you to fulfill His purpose for your life.

Prayer   *Father, help me see how my past experiences are preparing me for your purposes.*

 Discussion Questions

Think about your life as far as you can remember. What brought you extraordinary joy? _____

_____

_____

What things are you naturally good at? _____

_____

_____

Where were you living, and why? _____

_____

_____

What experiences helped shape who you are today? _____

_____

_____

What are your gifts, talents, and burdens? _____
_____
_____

What do you naturally gravitate to? _____
_____
_____

What are the things that you do that help you "feel God's pleasure?"_____
_____
_____

THOUGHTS

_____
_____
_____
_____
_____
_____
_____
_____
_____

Bloom Where You Are Planted

*If you have a skill, work at it and express it. In time,
people who have a fitting position will find you
(1 Samuel 16:16-18).*

16 Let our lord now command your servants who are before you to seek out a man who is skillful in playing the lyre, and when the harmful spirit from God is upon you, he will play it, and you will be well." 17 So Saul said to his servants, "Provide for me a man who can play well and bring him to me." 18 One of the young men answered, "Behold, I have seen a son of Jesse the Bethlehemite, who is skillful in playing, a man of valor, a man of war, prudent in speech, and a man of good presence, and the LORD is with him."

We all have dreams and wants in our hearts. In sports, coaches have what they call a "dream job," a team that they hope will be the last one they coach or a team they grew up idolizing and dreaming about. The reality is, we all have our dream job, but most of us are not in it. Some surveys indicate that as many as 70% of the workforce do not even like their current job, let alone work in their dream job.

How do we get our dream job? Leaders have a special responsibility here. They oversee people and should notice specific gifts and talents. Sometimes, these abilities are better served elsewhere. One prominent issue is to express these gifts and talents, and, in time, the needed position or post will find you.

David had many skills; one was being a talented musician. When a gifted musician was needed, David's name was mentioned. He played the harp so well that his reputation preceded himself. His gift was expressed, and an evil spirit no longer tormented Saul. Gifts and talents lead to serving and bettering others' lives. No job can bring true fulfillment if others are not blessed.

If you possess a gift, find a way to express it so you can build up connections, contacts, and a reputation. When there is a need to be filled, someone with experiential knowledge of your talents can connect you. In the journey of life, it is crucial to ask ourselves: what am I good at, and what do I enjoy doing? What are you passionate about or have a burden for? When these questions are in unison, God's will is likely present, and a dream job is found.

Prayer *Lord, help me not focus on any place but where I am at now. Help me give my best to whatever I am doing for your glory. Help my ambition not overtake my faith and help me be content where I am trusting that you can move me where I need to go.*

 Discussion Questions

Why do we often think the "grass is greener on the other side?" _____

_____

Entry-level jobs are fine. How can an attitude of giving it your all and trusting God with the rest give you more rest?

_____

_____

Are you happy where you are now? _____

_____

_____

If not, what are you hoping for?_____

_____

_____

THOUGHTS _____

_____

_____

_____

_____

_____

_____

A Talent Expressed Leads to Blessing

God gives us gifts and abilities to bless those in need.
It is crucial to discover the talents God has given us
and express them in the community.

1 Samuel 16:23: "Whenever the spirit from God came on Saul, David would take up his lyre and play. Then relief would come to Saul; he would feel better, and the evil spirit would leave him."

"He who knows others is wise; he who knows himself is enlightened."

—Lao Tzu

One big topic of discussion in the business world is the term EQ: Emotional Intelligence. Howard Gardner of Harvard describes EQ as: "Your EQ is the level of your ability to understand other people, what motivates them, and how to work cooperatively with them." [1]Many studying and writing about EQ argue that self-awareness and self-regulation are crucial to growing in EQ. Leaders must know their people and themselves. Though blind spots exist in all of us, a growth of who we are can only help in leading and serving people. One of the most important things for a productive leader and a worker is to know their gifts and abilities and be able to function within them.

David had a gift of music, playing the lyre in such a way that people around him were blessed. In the case of Saul, he suffered from a form of mental illness or depression that David's gift of playing the harp helps alleviate, soothing the king's soul. It is vital for leaders to discover the talents of their followers. Expressing their gifts brings health to those around them. Expressing your gifts and talents more regularly will produce personal happiness as well as happiness for others.

Do you have a gift but are not able to express it? Find a way independently to use your talents. Like David, who played the harp, people heard his musical talent, and eventually, God used it to prepare him to be king. David served Saul before he would take over for him.

What are some things you are good at? Think back as far as you can into childhood; what did you do well? What awards did you win? These questions and their answers can unlock the key to your gift to the world.

Prayer Lord, help me use the gifts and talents you have given me to grow your kingdom. Help me discover where I am gifted and us them for your glory.

See Romans 12:6-8; 1 Corinthians 12:8-10; Ephesians 4:11-12, and 1 Peter 4:11.

 Discussion Questions

What are some things you are good at? _____

_____

_____

Think back as far as you can into childhood. What did you do
well? _____

_____

What awards did you win? _____

_____

_____

What do you think are your spiritual gifts? _____

_____

_____

THOUGHTS
_____

_____

_____

_____

_____

_____

_____

_____

Blessing Your Boss

One metric of maturity is how we relate to authority. Relating to those in positions above us can be difficult. One area that people can grow in: try to bless those they report to.

1 Samuel 16:22: "Then Saul sent word to Jesse, saying, "Allow David to remain in my service, for I am pleased with him.""

One of the most important things to possess for success in life is maturity. Whether in work, marriage, romance, dating, friendship, or relationships with co-workers, success in life is proportional to proper development. One measure of maturity is how we relate to authority.

Oftentimes, those in leadership are easy to criticize. Their life and actions are public for all to see. Since all people are imperfect and all make mistakes, the leader's actions are for all to see and criticize. But blessing those over you is also important.

One crucial component of growth and maturity is how authority is dealt with. If someone continually has a problem of submitting to authority and always must rebel or not follow the rules, inherently, there exists a maturity problem. Blessing those in authority is biblical, for God has given authority as part of his structure. We are called to love all people, this includes our leaders, and we are specifically called to pray for our leaders (1 Timothy 2:1-2).

Not only is it biblical, but it could also help our career. Regardless of vocation advancement, our goal should be to love and glorify God. Sometimes it is hardest to love those in authority over us, but clearly, the Bible teaches that we should seek to bless everyone, including our bosses.

A quote attributed to Aristotle reads, "He who cannot be a good follower cannot be a good leader." Blessing our bosses maybe some of the best training for future leadership positions. Are you having trouble with someone who is over you? Say a prayer for them right now, asking God to bless them and help them grow in areas needed. Say a prayer for yourself, asking God to help you love your boss and for wisdom in how you can be a blessing to her or him.

Prayer *Father, forgive me if I have given authority a hard time. Help me do a better job of being a blessing to those I report to. Forgive me if I have not been a good follower, help me be humble and be a blessing.*

 Discussion Questions

We all have people we report to. Who are they? _____

_____

_____

Have I been a blessing to them? _____

_____

_____

What are the ways I can pray for those over me? _____

_____

_____

How can I encourage those who supervise me? _____

_____

_____

THOUGHTS

_____

_____

_____

_____

_____

_____

_____

Facing the Giants

Leaders face challenges that are beyond their ability to overcome. They are placed in situations where only God can get them through.

And there came out from the camp of the Philistines a champion named Goliath of Gath, whose height was six cubits and a span.
1 Samuel 17:4

Leadership means facing giants: challenges that are beyond a person's ability to overcome. Every leader will be confronted with decisions and circumstances that threaten their organization. These giants are terrifying because they can do extreme harm to many, not just the leader. They are also terrifying because they are difficult to overpower, scary, elicit fear in many, and seem unwinnable, but all giants can be overcome with God.

The story of David versus Goliath is one of the most famous stories in the Bible. Even those unfamiliar with Christianity or Judaism are no strangers. Goliath was a huge test for the nation of Israel. Some scholars have stated that Goliath could be upwards of nine feet tall, but clearly, he was of such physical stature that even King Saul, who was also quite tall, was no match.

Goliath was a champion, a fierce warrior, not just a tall, imposing figure. The challenge was so great that no one in Israel dared to face him. Giants are not giants unless you are up against a champion.

Left unchallenged, giants taunt. Day after day for 40 days (1 Samuel 17:16), Goliath reminded his enemies of their clear disadvantage, petrifying the nation. If left unopposed, this giant would eventually devour them. When giants are left unaddressed, they taunt and remind us of our deficits leading to fear (1 Samuel 17:24). For those who possess the bravery and courage to face the challenges head-on, dealing with the fears and insecurities of those who are afraid will be another giant to slay (1 Samuel 17:26-28). For some, the giants of life produce such fear that their courage becomes inert (17:33).

When spiritual giants threaten our lives, leaders must lean on God's power and remember His past faithfulness to lead them into present faith and courage (1 Samuel 17:34-37).

Prayer *There are many giants to face in my life. Help me not give in to my fears. Help me see that you are bigger than the giants that threaten me.*

 Discussion Questions

What are the things I am most afraid of? _____

_____

What prevents me from taking the final step? _____

_____

What giants are in my life now? _____

_____

What are some giants in the past or in history that have toppled people, companies, cultures, and rulers?_____

_____

THOUGHTS

Insecurely Threatened

Leaders must accept that others will be threatened by their leadership and will use lies, slander, and distortion as weapons against them.

"But when David's oldest brother, Eliab, heard David talking to the men, he was angry. "What are you doing around here anyway?" he demanded. "What about those few sheep you're supposed to be taking care of? I know about your pride and deceit. You just want to see the battle!"
1 Samuel 17:28

Leadership means dealing with people. It can be the greatest of joys or the worst heartaches. People are sinful, delicate, sensitive, and insecure, which can lead to irrational behavior. Human nature is easily threatened and will resort to attacking the source of the threat instead of taking responsibility through repentance, personal introspection, and examination.

One of the weapons that people use is slander. It is easier for the threatened person to change reality and smear someone else than to accept his or her own shortcomings and repent.

David is obeying his father's wish of bringing his brother's grain, bread, and cheese to the commander. When David arrives, he is appalled at the fear and cowardice displayed by Israel's army, enabling the Philistines to taunt them daily. This taunting spurs David to action. After hearing David inquire about the reward for killing the giant, displaying courage, and not being afraid of Goliath, David's older brother is deeply perturbed and attacks his youngest brother's character.

Maybe Eliab is still seething with jealousy because he was not chosen to be king (1 Samuel 16:7). Eliab was the oldest and most entitled to lead the family after his father dies; God's rejection could have bitterly stung. Maybe earlier, watching his youngest brother being anointed by the prophet produced in him envy that poisoned his heart (1 Samuel 16:13). Instead of graciously supporting his brother, Eliab attacks him (1 Samuel 17:28), accusing him of being arrogant and evil, unconcerned with the battle.

Eliab should already know that his youngest brother has faith that kills lions and bears, accompanied by a deep devotion. His family already knew of his reputation (1 Samuel 16:17-19), his older brother should have been supportive instead of combative.

Leaders must accept the fact that their very existence will make people feel uncomfortable, leading to personal attacks that unfairly smear their character and personhood.

Prayer *Lord, my very existence will make some people feel uneasy. They will fire arrows of anger, slander, and defamation. Help me see through their hurts and pains and offer grace.*

 Discussion Questions

Who am I struggling with right now? _____

_____

_____

Why does this person cause me angst? _____

_____

_____

Are my thoughts rational or irrational? _____

_____

_____

Think back to when someone slandered or lied about you. Why did they do it? _____

_____

_____

What causes people to be threatened? _____

_____

_____

What are the ways they use to protect themselves? _____

_____

_____

_____

Remember the Past to Help in the Present

Leaders will encounter enormous challenges that will be difficult to overcome. It is then that they need to meditate on God's past faithfulness in their lives. God's past faithfulness fuels present faith.

The LORD who rescued me from the paw of the lion and the paw of the bear will rescue me from the hand of this Philistine."
1 Samuel 17:37

Leadership means facing challenging conflicts, which almost never end. These conflicts arise as interpersonal conflicts, global pandemics, relationship conflicts, management struggles, uninspired followers, developing leaders, and leading an organization (to name a few). Other challenges like changes in the economy, finances, and trust also arise to create angst and stress for the leader. Many of the challenges appear from the outset as insurmountable giants.

David literally faced a "huge" challenge: a literal, not figurative, giant. Standing around nine feet tall, Goliath leveraged his height and strength to intimidate Israel. The only figure who could remotely oppose Goliath would be Saul, the only Israelite with an equally intimidating physique (1 Samuel 9:2).

For forty straight days, Goliath and the Philistines taunted the nation. Life's giant challenges often taunt us before we fight them. If they could be dealt with easily, they would present no challenge. Saul is at his whit's end. He knows that there is no one brave enough to fight Goliath. Morale is declining, compromising Israel's ability to win a battle against the giant and the Philistines. Saul knows defeat is imminent if nothing changes. The king is so distraught that when a young boy volunteers to fight the giant, Saul accepts. David had great confidence, accompanied by a child-like faith.

Likely fifteen years old but probably no older than twenty, David possesses a worldview that sees God's greatness. David remembered what God did for him in the past, delivering him from lions and bears. When the boy saw the giant, fear was overcome by faith. David knew Goliath was no match for the power of God and not an insurmountable challenge. It became a means for God to receive glory. God's past faithfulness should fuel our present faith, courageously leading us to the battle, not running away from it. God is bigger than these giants

Prayer *Father, help me not forget all the ways you have been faithful to me. I pray the past faithfulness fuels my present faith.*

 Discussion Questions

What challenges are you facing that will give God glory if they are overcome? _____

_____

Are there marital issues? _____

_____

Relationship struggles? _____

_____

Personal dryness? _____

_____

Money problems? Global problems?_____

_____

_____

How has God answered prayer? _____

_____

_____

How was He faithful in the past? _____

_____

_____

Was there a great need that He clearly provided for?_____

_____

_____

Call It Courage

Leaders need courage. A deep relationship with God leads to deep faith and courageous action, fueling and growing the bravery needed to overcome challenges.

45 Then David said to the Philistine, "You come to me with a sword and with a spear and with a javelin, but I come to you in the name of the LORD of hosts, the God of the armies of Israel, whom you have defied. 46 This day the LORD will deliver you into my hand, and I will strike you down and cut off your head. And I will give the dead bodies of the host of the Philistines this day to the birds of the air and to the wild beasts of the earth, that all the earth may know that there is a God in Israel, 47 and that all this assembly may know that the LORD saves not with sword and spear. For the battle is the LORD's, and he will give you into our hand."
1 Samuel 17:45-47

"People don't follow titles, they follow courage."~ William Brown[2]

This famous quote that was also cited in the famous blockbuster movie Braveheart teaches one of the absolute characteristics of leadership. Great leadership requires courage. Merriam-Webster's dictionary defines courage as the "mental or moral strength to venture, persevere, and withstand danger, fear, or difficulty."[3] David possessed a courage that was born out of his (a) youth, (b) experience, and (c) meditation on Scripture, which all fueled his growth and knowledge of God. We will now look at these three areas of David's life.

Youth. There is just something about being young, where one has great purity in future hope.

> "Truly, I say to you, unless you turn and become like children, you will never enter the kingdom of heaven. 4 Whoever humbles himself like this child is the greatest in the kingdom of heaven." —Matthew 18: 3-4

David possessed the eyes of youth that were not yet scared by life. As one gets older, the innocence of the world becomes compromised by its suffering and injustices. Youth, though most have been exposed to the world's cruelty, still possess a worldview that has not been overly tarnished by pain and trouble. David's youth allowed him to take God at his word and see God's work. The Bible says we must humble ourselves, like children, to see God for who he is.

Experience. Though David was a young man before he faced Goliath, he remembered all God had done for him. Before facing the giant in battle, he remembered how God delivered him when he fought lions and bears that were trying to harm his sheep. David did not forget what God had done for him in the past, and it fueled his present faith.

Meditation. There is much devotion to the word of God in the Psalms, but many of them are uncertain who the author is. Psalm 119 is the longest chapter in the entire Bible, consisting of

176 verses. Almost every single verse in Psalm 119 addresses the prominence of God's word. One Psalm that can be attributed to David is Psalm 19. David's passion for God's word is very clear and evident. The Bible says faith comes through hearing and hearing from the word of God (Romans 10:17). To grow one's faith, knowing and meditating on Scripture is essential.

> The law of the Lord is perfect, reviving the soul; the testimony of the Lord is sure, making wise the simple; 8 the precepts of the Lord are right, rejoicing the heart; the commandment of the Lord is pure, enlightening the eyes; 9 the fear of the Lord is clean, enduring forever; the rules of the Lord are true, and righteous altogether. 10 More to be desired are they than gold, even much fine gold; sweeter also than honey and drippings of the honeycomb. —Psalm 19:7-10

Clearly, David had a deep respect and love for the word of God, which delighted his heart and mind. Leaders need to cultivate courage, and this courage can grow if we deepen our walk with God. James Allen writes: "The physically courageous man conquers another in a fight; the morally courageous man conquers the opinions of many men, and wins thousands to his cause; but the divinely courageous man conquers the world, and his conquest is one of blessedness and peace, and not of bloodshed or party strife." John Maxwell writes, "A great leader's courage to fulfill his (or her) vision comes from passion, not position."⁴ To get this courage, one needs to be fueled by their passion and love for God.

Prayer Father, help me not see the world as I see it, but as you see it. Help me be disciplined to spend time knowing you so I can be brave when circumstances seem insurmountable.

Discussion Questions

What are the ways I can spend more time with God?

☐ Lunch break?

☐ Waking up earlier in the morning to read?

☐ Listening to the Bible while commuting to work?

☐ Listening to the Bible on my phone or CD?

What are some things God has done for me in the past that should help me face my current challenges? _____

_____

_____

THOUGHTS _____

_____

_____

_____

_____

Relationship Connections

*Leaders meet many people. Some people will form
a strong instant connection, while others will never
progress or remain contentious for no real reason.*

"The soul of Jonathan was knit to the soul of
David, and Jonathan loved him as his own soul. . . .
8 And Saul was very angry."
1 Samuel 18:1, 8

Leadership means relationships. Many of these relationships will be strictly professional, but all will involve some level of emotion. Relationships mean chemistry and connection. With some people, there will be a strong instant connection. With others, the chemistry and connection must develop over time. There are those relationships that will never progress beyond a specific emotional barrier. Finally, there are those relationships where you will not be liked for no real reason.

Leaders do not just lead individuals but also teams. For great leadership to occur, trust must be forged, which means relational connections. As with all relationships, the leader will form a more natural bond with some than with others. People may develop a deeper connection after talking with someone for five minutes than they have with someone else after five years.

Leverage the relationships that have formed an instant connection. There is no guarantee that in the long term, they will pan out or that relationships that have no early connections cannot form a fiduciary trust. Relationships are the essence of leadership and life. Energy output can be gauged by a relational connection. For David, Jonathan forged a deep bond, one that he would willingly abdicate his position as next in line for the throne because Saul could not stand his best friend David's success.

You will form connections that are instant and deep, while others will leave you feeling despised. Leaders need to focus on building relationships that bring life and limit those that bring despondency.

Prayer   *Lord, I meet many people. Help me identify those who give me life and those who take life away. Strengthen the bonds of life-giving relationships and limit life-draining ones.*

 Discussion Questions

Do you have a Jonathan in your life that is not your spouse? _

_____

_____

Who is he or she? _____

_____

_____

If not, should you be praying for one? _____

_____

_____

Are there people in other places outside my current office, community that could use accountability?_____

_____

_____

THOUGHTS
_____

_____

_____

_____

_____

_____

Spiritual Success

When God's hand is upon you, successful results follow.

"And David went out and was successful wherever Saul sent him, so that Saul set him over the men of war. And this was good in the sight of all the people and also in the sight of Saul's servants."
1 Samuel 18:5

Leadership means results. In an ecclesial setting, this can be difficult. In the world of business, results are a significant metric for the leader's success. A great deal of criticism has been laid at the church's feet for focusing too much on "business tactics" and "corporate America techniques." Harvard Business Review has replaced the Bible in some pastors' strategy implementation.

Some churches have been criticized for focusing too much on what the secular world does to garner success. If pastors are reading secular leaders, they could be criticized for being influenced by the world. But there is a lot to learn from people, regardless of their worldview. God reveals himself through the natural realm, not just supernatural. Creation all around testifies to his glory (Romans 1:20-21).

People use various definitions of success. One definition from Merriam-Webster is "favorable or desired outcome . . . the attainment of wealth, favor, or eminence."[5] In the end, spiritual success is a work of God. In Acts 5:34-39, Gamaliel, a Pharisee, counsels other Jewish leaders to leave the imprisoned apostles alone because if God is not in it, their plans will fail. 1 Corinthians 3:6 states that God causes growth. Throughout the books of Ezra and Nehemiah, the phrase "God's hand" is present. Clearly, spiritual success is a work of God.   David had this success through God. Whatever Saul asked him to do, David did it with success. Success can involve results and metrics, and in David's case, he won many battles over Israel's enemies.

Prayer Father, though I don't want to be obsessed with results, I know that part of glorifying you is to bear much fruit (John 15:8). Help me bear fruit for your glory.

 Discussion Questions

How can focusing on results distract us from walking with God? _____

_____

_____

How can we use results as a measure for God's leading and working? _____

_____

_____

What is the balance between results and faith? _____

_____

_____

_____

THOUGHTS _____

_____

_____

_____

_____

_____

_____

The Relational Consequences
of Spiritual Success

*When leaders succeed, some will be drawn to them
with deeper affection, while others will elicit fear.*

"And David had success in all his undertakings,
for the LORD was with him. 15 And when Saul saw
that he had remarkable success, he stood in fearful
awe of him. 16 But all Israel and Judah loved David,
for he went out and came in before them."
1 Samuel 18:14-16

Relationships are like magnets. When they come into contact with one another, they will either attract or repel. If the northern end of a magnet comes into contact with the southern end, a strong attraction can develop, but if either northern or southern ends of two magnets are in close proximity with the same northern or southern end of another magnet, repulsion happens.

People are similar to magnets. Our life elicits different emotions from people. Leaders must deal with whichever facet appears. Success is highlighted when God's hand is on the person.

Those closest to your position usually are the ones most threatened. Sometimes a leader's success shines a light on others' failure or unproductivity. Saul was king, but his insecurities led him to fear David instead of celebrating his success. He could not see that as long as the nation as well, he was well. David's success was a blessing to the nations, endearing their hearts toward their future king. Leaders must bless their followers, not be threatened by their success.

In an old western movie titled High Plains Drifter, Clint Eastwood utters a famous line on what causes people to fear:

> Sarah Belding: Be careful. You're a man who makes people afraid, and that's dangerous.
> The Stranger (Eastwood): Well, it's what people know about themselves inside that makes 'em afraid.

Saul was afraid of David's success when he should have been celebratory. It was what was on his inside that made him afraid of David.

Prayer — *Lord, help me root out all the envy, jealousy, bitterness, and anger in my life. Help me not feel threatened when others succeed but rejoice in their blessing.*

 Discussion Questions

Think of a time when someone succeeded and made you feel like a failure? _____

_____

_____

Think of a time when you succeeded, and someone else tried to attack you? _____

_____

_____

What causes this reaction in us? _____

_____

_____

What is it about ourselves that makes us afraid? _____

_____

_____

_____

What are the things inside of us that cause fear?_____

_____

_____

_____

Your Word Reveals Your Character

*Insecure people do not keep their word; they make
promises, but do not follow through.*

"Then Saul said to David, "Here is my elder
daughter Merab. I will give her to you for a wife. Only
be valiant for me and fight the LORD's battles." For
Saul thought, "Let not my hand be against him, but
let the hand of the Philistines be against him." . . .
But at the time when Merab, Saul's daughter, should
have been given to David, she was given to Adriel the
Meholathite for a wife.
1 Samuel 18:17, 19

Being attacked as a leader is part of the job. Because leaders
touch so many lives, their very presence touches the deepest
insecurities of immature souls. Because young souls attack, leaders
must remember that most of these attacks are a reflection of
the attacker, not the leader. Deep hurts and pains in the heart
of the attacker often are triggered by the leader's life for no
understandable reason.

One rule: if you are doing well in your life, someone around
you will feel threatened. Studies have revealed that many people
feel worse about themselves when they read social media. They
are fed a picture of someone's life going well, making them feel
like a failure.

Such is the life of the leader. Because they are in this position,
something must be making someone else feel bad. The threats

will usually come from someone right above you, someone who is your equal, or someone who is just a notch below. Location to the leader often correlates with the threat level, though attacks can come from anywhere. Mature people can handle this personal dissonance, but it is insecure people with less maturity that produce flight, fight, or fright behaviors.

One key to recognizing a potential threat is whether they keep their word. If they consistently promise things but do not follow through, this is a sign of immaturity. Saul made a promise to David but did not keep it. Insecure people say things but do not fulfill their obligations.

We all possess some degree of insecurity and struggle to keep our word, but when promises are made and not kept, this is the ultimate sign of someone who has character issues, something to keep an eye on. It is these people who will cause much stress.

Prayer *Father, may I honor the words I say. If I make a promise, help me keep it.*

 Discussion Questions

Why do so many people say things but never follow through?

_____

_____

_____

Why does this act of not following through make us feel so upset? _____

_____

_____

Has anyone ever promised something but did not fulfill their word? _____

_____

_____

THOUGHTS

_____

_____

_____

_____

_____

_____

Insecurity Leads to Irrationality

*When insecure people feel threatened, they become
irrational. When Saul's daughter fell in love with
David, Saul saw it as an opportunity to eliminate him.*

Now Saul's daughter Michal loved David. And
they told Saul, and the thing pleased him. 21 Saul
thought, "Let me give her to him, that she may be
a snare for him and that the hand of the Philistines
may be against him." . . . Now Saul thought to make
David fall by the hand of the Philistines.
1 Samuel 18: 20-21, 25

Leaders must deal with their personal demons, or these inner
fears will eventually destroy their ability to think clearly. Saul had
a deep-seated irrational fear of David. Seeing God's hand upon
David caused great fear in Saul's heart. A wise and secure leader
would recognize God's hand in David's life and rejoice. Any person
using God's gifts for the betterment of the organization – in this
case, a kingdom – is nothing but a win for everyone.

Saul could not overcome his hurts and fears. His fixation on
David was so all-encompassing that Saul became obsessed with
David's elimination. Ruthlessly, when his daughter fell in love
with David, Saul's skewed psyche seized upon an opportunity to
sabotage his rival. Fortunately, when God is moving, nothing can
stop Him. Wise spiritual leadership recognizes this and moves with
God. But when a leader's ego gets in the way, his wounded pride
cannot accept someone more successful than him.

Saul could not see God's hand, further adding to the threat. Insecure people do irrational things. An irrational perspective on life can spur normally wise leaders to exercise barbaric cruelty. Claiming a correct view of Scripture, they use the Bible to justify despicable violent acts. Time will eventually reveal the complete falsity of their logic.

Saul tried to eliminate his foe using his daughter as fodder. His obsession with killing his rival failed because God surrounded David with a layer of protection. Instead of focusing on your rival, concentrate on wrestling your own demons until you find peace. Saul could not do it, but we must or suffer the consequences.

Prayer *Lord, there are people that cause me to see my sin in ways that are too real. Help me see my own sin and confess so I can walk the path to healing.*

 Discussion Questions

Is there something preoccupying your thoughts and producing a negative impact on your job? Family? Relationships? Marriage?

_____

_____

_____

Are people questioning your mental health? _____

_____

_____

_____

_____

_____

_____

_____

_____

_____

_____

_____

_____

The Secret to Success

*When God's hand is on you, He will make your
results a success.*

Saul saw and knew that the LORD was with
David, . . .
Then the commanders of the Philistines came out
to battle, and as often as they came out David had
more success than all the servants of Saul, so that his
name was highly esteemed.
1 Samuel 18:28, 30

There is no real formula to assure God's hand will be upon you.
Walking with God is the best plan for success as a spiritual leader.

The good hand of his God was on him. 10 For Ezra had set his
heart to study the Law of the LORD, and to do it and to teach his
statutes and rules in Israel.

Ezra 7:9-10

For spiritual success to occur, leaders must be completely
immersed in the word of God, allowing His wisdom to guide every
decision.

Humans long to make a name for themselves, but in walking
obediently with God, He will make a name for them. Great
Christians have said: "Work as if everything depends on you but
pray as if everything depends on God." Though there is some truth
to this statement, and leaders must work hard, in the end, it is still
God's hand that brings.

If one searches the word "success" on the web, you will find things like "10 Steps to Success," "How to Succeed at Anything," and "7 Habits of Highly Successful People." How does one achieve real success? Clearly, from David's life, we must see where God is moving and go with him.

Saul knew this truth, but instead of humbly submitting to God's plan, he tried to change it. David was gifted, and he was very close to God while Saul was close to his ego. Is there someone beneath you in the flow chart that is doing an excellent job? Do they threaten you? Instead of trying to sully their name, embrace their success as your own and try to make the organization, you are part of greater success.

The Bible's way is to be close to God, know His word, live His word, and see where He is moving and move with him.

Prayer   *Help me submit to your plan, not force my own. Help stay close to you and hide your word in my heart. Allow me to see where you are moving and move with you.*

 Discussion Questions

What are the ways I can immerse myself in God's word more?

_____

_____

_____

What are clear tenants of scripture that I must follow?

_____

_____

_____

How can my life be more like Ezra's?_____

_____

_____

THOUGHTS

God Moves in People

God moves in other people's lives to help. Though there will be people who do not like us and desire our demise, there will be others who delight in us and will come to our aid.

And Saul spoke to Jonathan his son and to all his servants, that they should kill David. But Jonathan, Saul's son, delighted much in David.
1 Samuel 19:1

As we have discussed earlier, leadership means people. Some will despise us and desire our demise, but others will delight in us and desire to help. Leaders should be aware that about ten percent of their followers will follow them with complete devotion, while another ten percent will despise them. It is the middle 80% still choosing sides that must be influenced and leveraged. The top ten percent will be easily identified by their voluntary support and deep devotion to the leader.

Jonathan was a top tier person that a leader could count on. He had much to lose being David's friend. Number one, the kingship of Israel was rightly his. By being devoted to David, Jonathan was forfeiting his future. Jonathan clearly saw something in David, and God joined their hearts together in a deep friendship (1 Samuel 18:1).

Jonathan is highly regarded in the Bible, which is puzzling because Saul is so unfavorable. The old adage of the apple not falling far from the tree certainly does not apply to Jonathan. God clearly moved in Jonathan's life so he could see something special in David and something lacking in his father. He chose his friend over his father. Instead of envy and insecurity, Jonathan chose love and loyalty.

When God is moving in other people, we must work hard to fight jealousy and insecurity and choose joy and love. Leaders need people who are not threatened by their successful results but people who will come alongside them to help further the success. People who are willing to give of themselves so that the leader can be the best he or she can be.

Prayer
Father, thank you for those who support me with complete devotion, help me be more devoted to following you. Give me the wisdom to recognize whether or not people desire my good or my demise.

Discussion Questions

Why is it so important to know that people will be supportive and not have to worry about everyone? _____

_____

_____

Who are the people now that support me and want what's best? _____

_____

_____

THOUGHTS

_____

_____

_____

_____

_____

_____

_____

_____

_____

Don't Let Your Heart Be Hardened

*A hard heart prevents us from experiencing God's joy
and leads us away from God's purposeful journey.*

1 Samuel 10:10: "the Spirit of God rushed upon him (Saul)."
1 Samuel 19:23: "And the Spirit of God came upon him (Saul)."
1 Samuel 20:33 "But Saul hurled his spear at him to strike him. So Jonathan knew that his father was determined to put David to death."

Our heart is the seat of our affections. What it desires, it gravitates to. Our heart must be trained and changed because it possesses great evil (Jeremiah 17:9). God changes hearts through his spirit (1 Samuel 10:9), but we still make our own choices. A hard heart is one that can no longer accept the things of God and is obsessed with one's own thoughts and desires.

How does one deal with a hard heart? One way is to see us within God's creation. The vast enormity of God's created Universe will point to His greatness and humanities' minuteness (Job 42). When we allow our ego to control our thinking, our hearts harden to the things of God.

Our own Milky Way Galaxy is estimated to be 100,000 light-years across. A light-year is the distance light travels in one year, approximately 6 trillion miles. The nearest galaxy to our Milky Way is Andromeda. How far away is Andromeda from the Milky Way?

Over 2.5 million light-years away. Multiply 6 trillion by 2.5 million, and we get a distance beyond our comprehension.

Scientists estimate there are over 100 billion galaxies in our universe, and this is only due to technological advances. Some scientists believe that an increase in technology could lead to the discovery of another 100 billion to one trillion galaxies. As we begin to ponder the creation of God, it becomes quite clear that we are very small in the grand scheme of God's creation. No wonder God ranted about His created world when Job demanded answers. Once Job understood the magnanimous God he served, his questions dissipated (Job 38-42).

We see that Saul had a special filling of God's spirit twice. Despite this, Saul could not let go of his rage to kill David. Several opportunities arose, and there is evidence that Saul tried to change based on all these opportunities (1 Samuel 24:16-22), but he could not let go of his rage, fear, and jealousy of David, which eventually lead to his destruction (1 Samuel 31).

A hard heart leads to a path of darkness and destruction. Grace, truth, love, joy, and prayer are weapons to fight it. Seeing one's place in the grand scheme of God's creation can help us not be so focused on our own lives.

Prayer *Lord, please don't let my heart be hardened. Help me see you every day as the great God you are. Help me never try to elevate myself to where you are.*

 Discussion Questions

Think about science and the universe. How does the magnitude of the universe help us see God for who he is? _____

_____

_____

How does the vast greatness of the universe help us see how small we are? _____

_____

_____

How does the fact that this great God, who created this enormous universe, and loves us unconditionally, help our hearts not be hardened? _____

_____

_____

THOUGHTS _____

_____

_____

_____

_____

_____

_____

Devoted Friends

*Leaders must have people in their lives that
refresh them.*

"And Jonathan made David swear again by his
love for him, for he loved him as he loved his own
soul."
1 Samuel 20:17

Friends are one of the greatest weapons against soul depletion. When leadership brings on tiredness and weariness, a choice friend can revive the heart with soul stimulating fellowship and love. Encouragement is crucial for the long journey of leadership, and no better place can encouragement be found than in the presence of a devoted friend.

In the age of social media, the term "friend" has been watered down. The popular social media site Facebook allows a limit of 5,000 friends on one's personal page. People can comment and "Like" anything you post. Twitter is another forum where many people can follow you. As of this writing, entertainer Katy Perry had the most followers on Twitter, topping over one hundred million. But social media has shown to lead to depression. Watching other people's lives and their apparent good fortune leads us to feel our own lives are inadequate. Are social media contacts real friends? Do they really provide the soul-filling that our eternal heart desires? Do you have one real friend that would be willing to help out at no personal benefit to them? How are these friends made? There is a lot of research, but the Bible seems to indicate that God just brings them along.

Jonathan was such a friend to David. History has shown that leaders can be so paranoid that they would even assassinate their own family to stay in power. Saul's rage reached such a point that his actions could have killed his own son. David needed a friend, and he had one in Jonathan. Relationships are what bring true happiness and joy to life.

Prayer *Lord, give me friends like Jonathan was to David. Help me be a good friend to people. Thank you for the people you have already given me.*

 Discussion Questions

If there were one person outside of your family that you could spend time with right now, who would it be? _____

_____

_____

If you were lying on a hospital bed, whom would you call to say goodbye to? _____

_____

_____

Are there people that recharge you just by being around them? _____

_____

Are there people who drain you?_____

_____

_____

THOUGHTS _____

_____

_____

_____

_____

_____

Impactful Decisions

*Leaders make decisions, unfortunately, sometimes
the wrong ones, and have terrible repercussions for
those who are around the leader.*

"And David said to Ahimelech the priest, "The
king has charged me with a matter and said to me,
'Let no one know anything of the matter about which
I send you, and with which I have charged you.' I
have made an appointment with the young men for
such and such a place . . . 22:13 And Saul said to him,
"Why have you conspired against me, you and the son
of Jesse, . . . 14 Then Ahimelech answered the king,
"And who among all your servants is so faithful as
David, . . . 16 And the king said, "You shall surely die,
Ahimelech, you and all your father's house."
1 Samuel 21:2; 22:13, 14, 16

Leadership requires decision-making. The choices that are
made have ramifications far beyond the leader's personal circle.
The skills and intuition of making good decisions are paramount,
for these decisions impact many lives. From small organizations to
multinational corporations, leadership decisions have ramifications.
Suffering is the result of bad choices.

David is on the run from Saul and seeks refuge in the city of
Nob. There at Nob, he meets Ahimelek, the priest. David lies to
the priest, saying that Saul sent him on a mission, veiling Ahimelek
from the truth, leaving him vulnerable to Saul's wrath. When David
was fearful and threatened, he lied. Doeg, the Edomite, saw David
and quickly rushed off to tell King Saul.

Leaders must realize that spies for their enemies are lurking in the shadows. Upon hearing the news from Doeg, Saul rushes to Nob and confronts Ahimelek. Saul had no compassion that Ahimelek was lied to and acted as if David was under the blessing of the king. Upon the news that Ahimelek helped David, Saul killed him and all the other priests at Nob as well as women, children, and animals. What Saul could not do to the Amalakites, he did it to Nob.

Instead of obeying God in 1 Samuel 15 and utterly destroying the Amalekite nation, Saul almost wiped out the city of Nob, fueled by his own anger. Only Abiathar, Ahimelek's son, escaped to tell David the awful news. David knew it was his fault all this happened (1 Samuel 22:22). His decision to lie to Abiathar's father cost this innocent priest's son his whole family and city. Leaders make decisions; the wrong ones can have devastating consequences.

Prayer *In my decision-making, give me your wisdom and understanding. Help provide counselors so I can make the right decisions.*

 Discussion Questions

What are some decisions that you have made that have been the wrong one?_____

_____

_____

What did you learn from them? _____

_____

_____

What were some bad decisions made that impacted you for the negative? _____

_____

_____

What did you learn from those experiences? _____

_____

_____

THOUGHTS _____

_____

_____

_____

_____

_____

People before Rules

Rules are crucial for organizational purposes. They help people understand expectations, boundaries, and structure, but rules should never take precedence over caring for others.

But the priest answered David, "I don't have any ordinary bread on hand; however, there is some consecrated bread here—provided the men have kept themselves from women." 5 David replied, "Indeed women have been kept from us, as usual whenever I set out. The men's bodies are holy even on missions that are not holy. How much more so today!" 6 So the priest gave him the consecrated bread, since there was no bread there except the bread of the Presence that had been removed from before the Lord and replaced by hot bread on the day it was taken away.
1 Samuel 21:4-6: 4

We need rules, but leaders must place a higher value on love than legalism. They are essential for any organization to function at its maximum capacity. Rules provide structure, direction, accountability, and clearly stated expectations for all to follow. They alert us to potential danger and shield us from harm. However, when rules are violated, consequences follow.

There are times when rules may conflict with our highest goal: caring for others. If a rule prevents a person's needs from being met or makes someone feel unimportant and undervalued, the application of the rule must be reassessed.

In 1 Samuel 21, David's men were hungry, but all Ahimelek the priest could offer them for sustenance was consecrated bread. Common people did not intend this bread for use. It was to be placed on a table in the tabernacle as an offering for the Lord. The twelve pieces of bread represented Israel's continual consecration to God, a reminder that God had provided for them (Exodus 25:30). Consecrated bread was to be set before the Lord on behalf of the nation of Israel as a lasting covenant (Leviticus 24:8). It was meant for the priests to eat only in the sanctuary of the Lord (Leviticus 24:9).

Ahimelek understood God's rules. He knew the purpose of consecrated bread being eaten by priests before the Lord was a reminder to the people of God's ongoing presence in the life of Israel. Yet, Ahimelek bent the rules so hungry people could be fed. People prevailed over proxy.

Jesus turns to this story, found in Matthew 12:3-4, Mark 2:23-27, and Luke 6:1-5, to counter the legalism of the Pharisees. According to Jewish law, harvesting was not to be conducted on the Sabbath, yet Jesus and his disciples walked through the fields picking heads of grain. The Pharisees rebuke them for their disobedience, but Jesus responds with vigor, using this story of David as an example.

Jesus teaches that the letter of the law does not take precedence over the spirit. Just as Ahimelek's feeding of the bread of Presence to hungry people did not violate the spirit of the law, Jesus's harvesting a few heads of grain for hungry people was not unlawful.

> Rules are crucial. Even Paul affirms the usefulness of the law (e.g., Galatians 3:19). However, the law is not paramount – Loving God and people is (John 15:12; Romans 13:8).

Prayer *Lord, my priorities today are to love you and love people, fill me with your spirit to give me the power to do so. Though rules are important and essential, love is more important. Help me to love while still carrying out the rules.*

 Discussion Questions

Are there any rules that you think get in the way of love or caring? _____

_____

_____

Is your organization more a rules-based environment where you feel "used and abused," or do you believe the organization cares for you? _____

_____

_____

Has anyone ever hurt you, or have you ever hurt someone else by following the letter of the law rather than its spirit? _____

_____

_____

_____

Danger Dodger

*Leaders must be able to sense coming danger and act
in a way to avoid it.*

And David rose and fled that day from Saul and
went to Achish the king of Gath. 11 And the servants
of Achish said to him, "Is not this David the king of
the land? Did they not sing to one another of him
in dances, 'Saul has struck down his thousands, and
David his ten thousands?'"

12 And David took these words to heart and
was much afraid of Achish the king of Gath. 13 So
he changed his behavior before them and pretended
to be insane in their hands and made marks on the
doors of the gate and let his spittle run down his
beard. 14 Then Achish said to his servants, "Behold,
you see the man is mad. Why then have you brought
him to me? 15 Do I lack madmen, that you have
brought this fellow to behave as a madman in my
presence? Shall this fellow come into my house?"
1 Samuel 21:10-15: 10

Leaders must see danger coming before it engulfs their
followers. Earth is an unsafe place. A quote attributed to Albert
Einstein reads: "The world is a dangerous place to live; not because
of the people who are evil, but because of the people who don't
do anything about it."[6]

We live in a world that produces suffering and harm in an
instant. With 86,400 seconds in each day, it only takes one second
for danger to hurl its spear of destruction at an unsuspecting victim.

From natural causes, human depravity, or human negligence, this planet is a perilous home.

Animals were given instincts and adaptations to help them avoid danger, organizations write safety plans and protocols in the event of peril, schools practice emergency drills, and the government exercises war games – all because the world is unsafe.

Leaders must be able to sense coming danger and be prepared with a plan for survival. Clearly, the Bible teaches that one result of sin is a more hazardous living environment. From natural disasters (Joel 2) to the evil done by one person to another, to personal struggles with our own flesh – there are many dangers that can harm us. A leader is one who foresees this danger and prepares his or her people to keep them safe.

David saw that he would be threatened by his reputation. He was already on the run from one king and now needed another for safety. But he could sense that the king of Gath would not welcome him and could feel threatened by David's reputation as a military conqueror more gifted than Saul. So, David proceeded to pretend he had lost his mind. After the king of Gath saw this, he no longer feared David and let him leave Gath unharmed. Leaders must see danger and prepare to protect themselves and their people from it.

Prayer Lord, give me the eyes to see what could hurt my people in the future and how to prepare to keep them safe.

 Discussion Questions

How can lessons learned from things like economics, war, and business help us see the danger? _____

_____

_____

What are some areas of potential danger, like a natural disaster or illness, for which we can begin planning preventative measures now? _____

_____

_____

THOUGHTS _____

_____

_____

_____

_____

_____

_____

Reputation Precedes Position

Your work is a collection of activities that lead to achievements. After a while, what you have done forms your reputation, which people may have heard about long before they know you.

1 Samuel 21:11: 11 But the servants of Achish said to him, "Isn't this David, the king of the land? Isn't he the one they sing about in their dances:
"'Saul has slain his thousands,
. . . . and David his tens of thousands?'"

Leadership is defined as activity that leads to achievement. Goals must be set and accomplished. Just to be active is not enough. There must be accomplishments. What we have produced establishes our reputation. After a while, people know about our reputation before they actually know us.

Ambition can become distracting if the main desire is to advance our personal reputation instead of the kingdom of God, but, in and of itself, advancing is not wrong. We all have dreams. But when dreams supersede the kingdom, they become a hindrance to our faith.

But some of these dreams involve growing and advancing in our occupational life. Promotions, higher pay, better positions are all part of the dream. We enter at an entry-level position, but many of us desire to be advanced. Sometimes that involves changing companies, changing places, and changing roles. Others will strike out as entrepreneurs.

Whether it's business, academics, recreation, science, or Christian ministry, one possesses a reputation. Over time, this reputation will arrive in places before you. There is great truth to the old adage: "Your reputation precedes you." Not everyone will think highly of you.

The best thing we can do is to give our all wherever we are. The future will take care of itself if we are doing a good job. Saul wanted to kill David because he felt a threat to his kingship. When we compare Saul's reputation to David's, Saul was not as respected or admired as David. This caused great dissonance in his soul.

Upon examination of the life of Saul, we see he earned his reputation. However, reviewing David's reputation and accomplishments, it is clear why the crowds would chant: "'Saul has slain his thousands, and David his tens of thousands?'"

Prayer *Lord, help me be like David, someone focused on pleasing you more than pleasing people. Help me not desire to get my "dream job" or be in another position, but help me focus on where you have me now. May my life reflect Christ to others, and may my reputation bring you glory and honor. May I trust you to lead and promote me.*

 Discussion Questions

Think back to the early years of work. What could you have done better? _____

_____

_____

Have you ever been in one position, job, or ministry, but had your eye on something else? _____

_____

_____

What are things we can do and change today that will help our reputation in the future? _____

_____

_____

THOUGHTS _____

_____

_____

_____

_____

_____

_____

The Cave of Character

Before David became king, he lived in a cave. Before God uses you greatly, he will break you to grow your character in preparation for his purposes.

1 Samuel 22:1 "David left Gath and escaped to the cave of Adullam."

Before God uses someone mightily, he must break his or her will. The great writer and speaker, A.W. Tozier, said, "It is doubtful whether God can bless a man greatly until He has hurt him deeply."

Character is formed through suffering (Romans 5:1-8). Before David became king of Israel, he lived in a cave. On the run, fearing for his life, David found a sanctuary where bears, snakes, and all sorts of wild animals live. Before God uses someone mightily, he breaks him or her. Jesus endured suffering too. Before Jesus began his ministry, he fasted forty days and nights in the wilderness and endured Satan's most severe temptations.

David is considered the greatest king of Israel. Jews believe he is the prototype of the Messiah. But before David takes the throne of Israel, he must live in a cave. The great political leader and anti-apartheid activist Nelson Mandela spent 27 years in jail for his desire to end the segregation going on in South Africa. One could consider this one of the greatest travesties in life. Such a brilliant man and leader was the victim of such a great injustice. On Mandela's time in jail, Desmond Tutu writes:

"But his anger was never greater than his patience or forgiveness. People say, look at what he achieved in his years in government – what a waste those 27 years in prison were. I maintain his prison term was necessary because when he went to jail, he was angry. He was relatively young and had experienced a miscarriage of justice; he wasn't a states person ready to be forgiving: he was commander-in-chief of the armed wing of the party, which was quite prepared to use violence.

The time in jail was quite crucial. Of course, suffering embitters some people, but it ennobles others. Prison became a crucible that burned away the dross. People could never say to him: "You talk glibly of forgiveness. You haven't suffered. What do you know?" Twenty-seven years gave him the authority to say, let us try to forgive."[7]

David endured a similar situation. When we endure suffering, we want immediate relief, like the Israelites who wandered the wilderness under Moses. Some wanted to go back to Egypt (Numbers 14:4-5), while others tried to enter the Promised Land before the appointed time (Numbers 14:40-45). We don't want to suffer. But God's path of character growth is suffering. Before David assumed the throne of Israel, he lived in a cave on the run from a powerful man who was trying to kill him. He slept where wild animals and reptiles dwelt so he could someday be the king that the chosen people of God would model as their future Messiah.

Prayer *Lord, help me not be worrisome about the cave of character when I know time spent dwelling there will prepare me for your next task of service. May the suffering I am experiencing now grow my heart and soul so that I can be more effective for your glory.*

 Discussion Questions

Think of a time where you experienced great suffering. How did it help you grow? _____

_____

_____

How did this experience prepare you for future effectiveness?

_____

_____

_____

Why is leaving the cave of character too early so detrimental to your future? _____

_____

_____

What experiences have shaped your character the most?

_____

_____

_____

The Cave of Preparation

Leaders are not wasting time during their period of waiting. It is during this time that God is working and molding the leader into someone he will use.

1 Samuel 22:1-2: David left Gath and escaped to the cave of Adullam. When his brothers and his father's household heard about it, they went down to him there. 2 All those who were in distress or in debt or discontented gathered around him, and he became their commander. About four hundred men were with him.

God prepares people for service. Though having character is crucial, skill is also tantamount. The best way to prepare a leader is to develop his or her character, but during this time, there will also be opportunities to grow in skill and experience. While David is fleeing for his life from Saul's desire to kill him, he hides and lives in a cave, but time in a cave did not prevent David from gaining experience in leading people. While he is hiding in a cave, his followers begin to grow. The text says that those who were also in distress or in debt or discontented gathered around him, and he became their commander. Even though he is hiding in a cave and fleeing for his life, David will now lead four hundred men.

Not only is he gaining experience to be the second king of Israel and the prototype of the Messiah, but this band of men will also form a core for his future military might. The number of followers eventually increases another two hundred, bringing his total strength to six hundred by the time they leave the cave of Adullam.

This original royal army will fight its first battle together against the Philistines at Keilah (1 Samuel 23:13). Throughout the remainder of 1 Samuel, this band of six hundred men faithfully follows David to victory. Despite David hiding out in a cave, God gives him opportunities to lead. The experience he gains leading this victorious band of six hundred (2 Samuel 8), is part of the preparation process for David to lead Israel.

Though we know, it was the Lord who gave David victory everywhere he went (2 Samuel 8:6); clearly, God used this time where hundreds of men joined him in a cave – and, later, more men in Keilah – as a time of training and preparation. David reigns as Israel's greatest king until Christ assumes the throne as the last king of Israel one thousand years later.

Prayer *Lord, help me not be impatient for the next position but help me see how the cave in which I am waiting is preparing me for your next assignment. Help me see how the circumstances around me are drawing me closer to you and helping me grow in skill and integrity.*

Discussion Questions

Think about life now. Are you where you want to be, or do you have your eye on something else? _____

_____

_____

How would getting to where you want to be too fast be detrimental? _____

_____

_____

How are you growing and changing now? _____

_____

_____

_____

_____

THOUGHTS _____

_____

_____

_____

_____

_____

_____

Bad Leaders Cause Innocent Suffering

*Leadership means influence. Every decision a leader
makes has a direct effect on others. An insecure
leader will often make bad decisions out of his or her
insecurities with the goal of protecting themselves but
at the expense of hurting others.*

1 Samuel 22:6, 9, 16, 18-19: Now Saul heard that
David and his men had been discovered. . . . But Doeg
the Edomite, who was standing with Saul's officials,
said, "I saw the son of Jesse come to Ahimelek son
of Ahitub at Nob. . . . the king said, "You will surely
die, Ahimelek, you and your whole family." . . . The
king then ordered Doeg, "You turn and strike down
the priests." So Doeg the Edomite turned and struck
them down. That day he killed eighty-five men who
wore the linen ephod. 19 He also put to the sword
Nob, the town of the priests, with its men and women,
its children and infants, and its cattle, donkeys and
sheep.

Life consists of decision making, and leaders make many
decisions. We must guard against making choices for our own self-
interests because unwise decisions have damaging consequences.
These consequences are heightened when they are made at the
price of another person's well-being. These types of decisions have
an impact on many.

When decisions are made that are provoked by insecurity, an unacceptable outcome is almost assured. Saul felt so threatened by David that he took his anger out against the priests. He felt they were committing treason against him by helping David. First, he accused the priest, Ahimelek, of conspiring against him, aiding David to kill Saul (1 Samuel 22:11). Saul is paranoid and does not see the truth. In fact, David will have two opportunities to kill Saul and will choose not to (1 Samuel 24 and 1 Samuel 26).

Ahimelek disagrees with Saul's assessment and affirms David's noteworthiness and loyalty to Saul, but Saul will have nothing to do with this rhetoric. When leaders are paranoid, they seek to eliminate the threat. Saul then twists the truth to justify his order to have the priests killed. He accuses the priests of lying and protecting David: "They knew he was fleeing, yet they did not tell me." In fact, the evidence is unclear whether they knew David's circumstances at all.

The priest was afraid when David came. To make matters worse, David lied and said he was on a secret mission from Saul (1 Samuel 21:2). This did not mitigate Saul's anger; he felt the priest was on David's side. Because of the king's insecurity, Ahimelek, eighty-five others who served God in the sanctuary, and the town of Nob fell victim to Saul's rage and were innocently killed. Insecure leaders are easily threatened and manipulate reality to justify their actions.

In what areas of our lives do we feel threatened? How are we manipulating reality to justify our decisions? These types of challenges often arise when we are in emotional distress. Our decisions matter and often impact more than just ourselves. The greater the influence, the more important it is to make the right decision. Are there people or things in our lives that make us uneasy or uncomfortable? Turn them over to the Lord and ask him to help.

 Lord, there are a lot of things out there, and a lot of people out there that do not make me feel safe. Help me trust in you to uphold me and not myself. Give me wisdom (James 1:5) to make the right decisions.

 Discussion Questions

What are some decisions that were made by others, especially those over you, that have affected you negatively? _____

_____

_____

_____

Has anyone ever been threatened by you and tried to have you, fired, or otherwise tarnish your reputation? _____

_____

_____

_____

What are some decisions you have made that have caused you distress? _____

_____

_____

Excuses Are Unacceptable

Leaders will fail and make wrong decisions. They can try to make excuses or confess their faults. Excuses are often a sign of an unfit leader, while confessions points to fitness.

1 Samuel 22:20-22: 20 But one son of Ahimelek son of Ahitub, named Abiathar, escaped and fled to join David. 21 He told David that Saul had killed the priests of the Lord. 22 Then David said to Abiathar, "That day, when Doeg the Edomite was there, I knew he would be sure to tell Saul. I am responsible for the death of your whole family."

Life involves making mistakes and rebounding from our failures. Leadership involves accepting our failures and confessing our faults. Leaders are not perfect and cannot make every decision correctly. Whether it is hiring the wrong person, making the wrong partnership, implementing a wrong program, executing a strategy incorrectly, hurting a person, offering improper advice, or cutting corners, leaders inevitably will make some wrong decisions.

Our typical response to doing something wrong or not doing what we are supposed to be to make excuses. When God confronted Adam over his sin, he immediately blamed Eve (Genesis 3:12). Cain killed his brother in a jealous rage and then snapped back when being confronted by God: "Am I my brother's keeper (Genesis 4:9)?" Moses made so many excuses that God's anger burned against him (Exodus 4:14), and his brother Aaron ended up having to help (Exodus 4:15-16).

Our founding fathers knew a little bit about excuses, George Washington said, "It is better to offer no excuse than a bad one." Ben Franklin said, "He that is good for making excuses is seldom good for anything else."

One could predict Saul's early demise when confronted by Samuel for having offered the sacrifice without waiting for the prophet. Saul replied in 1 Samuel 13:11-14:

> "When I saw that the men were scattering and that you did not come at the set time and that the Philistines were assembling at Michmash, 12 I thought, 'Now the Philistines will come down against me at Gilgal, and I have not sought the Lord's favor.' So, I felt compelled to offer the burnt offering." 13
>
> "You have done a foolish thing," Samuel said. "You have not kept the command the Lord your God gave you; if you had, he would have established your kingdom over Israel for all time. 14 But now your kingdom will not endure; the Lord has sought out a man after his own heart and appointed him ruler of his people because you have not kept the Lord's command."

Excuses reveal our priorities and passions or our lack thereof. If something had to be done and wasn't, our priorities are manifest. If we consistently make excuses at our work or ministry, they may reveal a misplaced passion. We often use the excuse, "I don't have time," when, in reality, it is a statement of value. If we really value something, we make time for it.

Everyone makes mistakes and fails at some point. These opportunities are the best tools for learning. How we respond to failure reveals a lot about who we are. Leaders must own up to their mistakes and accept they are wrong and not try to cover it with an excuse.

 *Father, help me be aware that making excuses reveals more about my character than it does about my competence. Help me be humble enough to admit I was wrong when I fail.*

 Discussion Questions

We have all been around people who make excuses. What makes this appear so unattractive? _____

_____

_____

_____

Think about the excuses we make. Are they legitimate, or do they reveal a deeper issue of passion and priorities? _____

_____

_____

_____

Our Decisions Influence Others Beyond Our Lives

Leaders make decisions, and these decisions have ram-
ifications on others' lives long after we are gone. Eli's
unfaithfulness led to the killing of the priests at Nob.

1 Samuel 2:29, 31-32: Why do you scorn my sacrifice and offering that I prescribed for my dwelling? Why do you honor your sons more than me by fattening yourselves on the choice parts of every offering made by my people Israel?'

The time is coming when I will cut short your strength and the strength of your priestly house, so that no one in it will reach old age, and you will see distress in my dwelling. Although good will be done to Israel, no one in your family line will ever reach old age. 33 Every one of you that I do not cut off from serving at my altar I will spare only to destroy your sight and sap your strength, and all your descendants will die in the prime of life.

Life means making choices. Leadership involves making decisions that impact the lives of those who follow. The story of Eli illustrates how decisions have ramifications years after our lifetime.

Many Old Testament scholars believe that the slaughter of the priests of Nob was a fulfillment of the prophecy God made against Eli years earlier when Samuel was young. Eli ended up being a very sorry Old Testament character whose evil sons caused great pain to others. Because of Eli's poor choices, he was cursed beyond his own time. Later, others would suffer as well.

God had prophesied that Eli's decision would affect the rest of his lineage, and the death of the priests at Nob (1 Samuel 22:6-19) may reflect partial fulfillment of this promise. Clearly, the decisions of our leaders have a far-reaching impact that can influence generations to come. Leaders must not take decision making lightly because the ramifications could harm others in the future.

Prayer   *Father, help me not be like Eli, who put his priorities over his family's and eventually you. Give me wisdom and understanding as I navigate through the cave of decision making.*

Discussion Questions

Has there ever been a decision in your childhood that negatively affected you into adolescence and adulthood?

_____

_____

What decisions in your company, country, or organization have given negative consequences today? _____

_____

_____

Which decisions yielded positive outcomes? _____

_____

_____

THOUGHTS

_____

_____

_____

_____

_____

_____

_____

_____

Careful Sharing

What leaders share, when they share it, and with whom they share, must be guarded. Any info that an enemy receives will be used against you.

1 Samuel 21:7 " Now one of Saul's servants was there that day, detained before the Lord; he was Doeg the Edomite, Saul's chief shepherd."

1 Samuel 22:22:" 22 Then David said to Abiathar, "That day, when Doeg the Edomite was there, I knew he would be sure to tell Saul. I am responsible for the death of your whole family."

Leaders have enemies. Not everyone who follows you will be loyal. In fact, some will try to undermine you while believing they are doing the right thing, even claiming they have a calling from God to remove you as if they are law enforcement officers reading you your Miranda rights.

The desire to bring about a leader's demise may stem from factors unrelated to the leader, i.e., a person's own issues of insecurity, their personal issues of relationship and authority, issues from childhood that exist but have not been dealt with. Leaders somehow can rub up against our blind spots, causing irrational behavior.

There are others who are loyal to another and misuse this feeling of loyalty by trying to usurp the leader. No one can serve two masters; he will hate one and love the other.

David went to Nob and sought help from Ahimelek, the priest. Though Ahimelek trembled in David's presence, he agreed to help and provided bread from the tabernacle and weaponry—the sword of Goliath—that David had killed. There was no sword like it.

While David asked Ahimelek for help, Doeg was taking mental notes and later reported to Saul everything he saw and heard (1 Samuel 22:9-10). Upon learning of these acts, Saul summoned Ahimelek. Following a confrontation with the priest, Saul ordered the death of not just Ahimelek, but all of the priests, and then the whole town.

Because David shared his thoughts in the presence of Doeg, a Saul supporter, others suffered. Leaders have enemies, and everything that is shared can be used against them. Thomas á Kempis, in The Imitation of Christ, wrote, "Do not open your heart to everyone, but discuss your affairs with one who is wise and fears God." Be careful with whom you disclose things to and be aware of who else is listening.

Prayer   *Father, give me wisdom and discernment to share with the right people, not those who would betray my confidence and seek to undermine me. Guard me against my enemies like you did King David over his time as Israel's shepherd.*

 Discussion Questions

How has gossip hurt you? _____
_____
_____

How have you gossiped about someone else? _____
_____
_____

What are some safeguards you can use to protect yourself from those who would share the info with your enemies?
_____
_____

THOUGHTS

_____
_____
_____
_____
_____
_____
_____
_____
_____

Holy Inquiry

*Because of the many decisions that must be made,
inquiring about the Lord's wisdom is crucial.*

1 Samuel 23:1-6: When David was told, "Look, the Philistines are fighting against Keilah and are looting the threshing floors," 2 he inquired of the Lord, saying, "Shall I go and attack these Philistines?"

The Lord answered him, "Go, attack the Philistines and save Keilah." 3 But David's men said to him, "Here in Judah we are afraid. How much more, then, if we go to Keilah against the Philistine forces!" 4 Once again David inquired of the Lord, and the Lord answered him, "Go down to Keilah, for I am going to give the Philistines into your hand." 5 So David and his men went to Keilah, fought the Philistines and carried off their livestock. He inflicted heavy losses on the Philistines and saved the people of Keilah. 6 (Now Abiathar, son of Ahimelek, had brought the ephod down with him when he fled to David at Keilah.)

Leaders always face tough decisions. For the Christian spiritual leader, prayer is essential. In this passage, David is unsure if he should lead his troops to battle, so he asks God. David's men were uncertain, so David asked the Lord again. Both times, God affirmed David that going into battle was what he wanted. So unlike Saul, who gave into the opinions of others, David obeyed the Lord. Because of David's obedience, God gave his future king victory.

Nehemiah was so sad over the walls of Jerusalem being burned down that he wept, mourned, and prayed (Nehemiah 1:4). Then, when bringing King Artaxerxes wine, the king noticed Nehemiah's sad demeanor and asked him the cause (Nehemiah 2:1-2). Before Nehemiah answered, he said a very quick prayer (Nehemiah 2:4). When Ezra was overwhelmed by the intermarriage of the postexilic nation of Israel, he prayed (Ezra 9:6-15). Prayer was not unique to Nehemiah and Ezra, Jesus frequently prayed, and Paul's prayers are well documented throughout his letters. One can argue that all 66 books of the Bible record a prayer or have some mention, connection, and reference to prayer.

Studying the Gospels, we find a significant amount of material dedicated to the prayer life of Jesus. Before he selected his disciples, he was all night in prayer. Before he would go to the cross, he sweated drops of blood and prayed to his Father if there was another way. S.D. Gordon writes in Quiet Talks on Prayer:

> How much prayer meant to Jesus! It was not only his regular habit, but his resort in every emergency, however slight or serious. When perplexed, he prayed. When hard pressed by work, he prayed. When hungry for fellowship, he found it in prayer. He chose his associates and received his messages upon his knees. If tempted, he prayed. If criticized, he prayed. If fatigued in body or wearied in spirit, he had recourse to his one unfailing habit of prayer. Prayer brought him unmeasured power at the beginning and kept the flow unbroken and undiminished. There was no emergency, no difficulty, no necessity, no temptation that would not yield to prayer.[8]

From the Old Testament through the New, throughout the Scriptures, prayer is preeminent.

Prayer was and is essential in the lives of prominent Christians. Leaders need to be constantly in prayer. Martin Luther prayed three hours a day. The life of the Christ-follower flourishes in peace, joy, and discernment when prayer is foremost. Seek and inquire of God often. Like David, people will not always be able to see what God is doing, but inquiring God for direction will eventually lead to the correct path.

 *Lord, may I remember to inquire of you for any big decision. May my life grow in prayer more and more.*

Discussion Questions

Why do I prioritize my work and responsibilities over prayer? .

_____

_____

_____

Are there creative ways I can pray more? _____

_____

_____

_____

Are their efficient ways prayer can be part of my life? _____

_____

_____

_____

What are some big decisions coming up that I must be in prayer over? _____

_____

_____

THOUGHTS

_____

_____

_____

_____

_____

_____

_____

_____

_____

_____

_____

_____

_____

Performance before Titles

*Leaders often will perform their jobs before they
receive the official title they will hold.*

1 Samuel 23:5: 5 So David and his men went to
Keilah, fought the Philistines and carried off their
livestock. He inflicted heavy losses on the Philistines
and saved the people of Keilah.

The Bible teaches that if you are faithful in little things, God
can entrust you with bigger responsibilities (Luke 16:10). People's
strengths, gifts, and aptitudes can often be discerned at an early
age. It is crucial we serve in the areas of our gifts and talents, for
we are fearfully and wonderfully made (Psalm 139:14). It is not
uncommon that leaders will perform their job responsibilities
before actually receiving the job. The two presidents that followed
George Washington—John Adams and Thomas Jefferson— went
straight to the office after being the Vice president. Head football
coaches were once assistants. CEO's often began as entry-level
workers. Officers in the military must rise to the position of general.

Leaders often perform the tasks of the leadership position
prior to ascension. Before David became king, he led his army to
battle and defeated the Philistines at Keilah. David's men were
afraid, causing David to inquire twice of the Lord. After God gave
David his instruction, David led his men to victory. This is one of
many battles that David and his men will win, but this one occurred
before he became king.

Prayer *Lord, help me see those who are already doing the work without the position and advocate for proper placement. Help me be patient if I am performing a task of a different position without the title and authority.*

Discussion Questions

Are there people to whom you have delegated tasks doing a great job? _____

_____

_____

Are there people in your organization who are already doing the work and shining at that task? _____

_____

_____

Keep an eye on them; they could be used in an important position in the future. Do you acknowledge their efforts?

_____

_____

THOUGHTS _____

_____

_____

_____

Unholy Excuses

*Leaders who are living in an unholy manner will use
God as an excuse for their unholy actions.*

1 Samuel 23:7: 7 Saul was told that David had gone to Keilah, and he said, "God has delivered him into my hands, for David has imprisoned himself by entering a town with gates and bars."

Leaders cannot make excuses. Former Governor of Massachusetts and Utah senator, Mitt Romney, once said, "Leadership is about taking responsibility, not making excuses." But people are sinful and sometimes continue in a sinful life. One sign that people are living this way is that they use God to justify their actions or falsely attribute things to God. Using God as an excuse sounds like this: "It's God's will _____

_____ (for me to do something that is motivated by my selfish, self-protective agenda)," but we know that it is sinful. Some people say that it is okay to be unethical because it is "God's will." Wrong! God's will never contradict God's word, but many people will bypass God's word to justify their sinful actions.

Saul is living in sin and feels threatened by David's success. He feels so threatened that the only way he believes he can enjoy any level of peace is to kill David. Even though David has the opportunity to kill Saul, he does not; whereas, Saul invests all of his energy into stopping David.

Here, in this scene, after David saves the town of Keilah from the Philistines, Saul receives news of David's whereabouts and believes God has delivered David into his hands to be killed. Saul pursued David hard and was closing in on him, but just before Saul could overtake David and his men, the king was diverted by news of the Philistines raiding the land. Saul broke away and departed to face the Philistines while David and his men were able to get away to the stronghold of En Gedi (1 Samuel 23:26-29).

Mother Angelica, Catholic nun, television personality, and a spiritual encourager to people like Rick Warren, says: "Man can and does rationalize his sins. He finds reasons for all his weakness, invents excuses that first calm, and then deadens his conscience. He blames God, society, education, and the environment for his wrongdoing."[9]

We all struggle with sin, and one of the struggles is to live in a false reality where we believe our actions are not wrong, but for God. Using God to justify sin is the ultimate unholy excuse, and leaders are especially susceptible to this temptation due to the enormous number of decisions they make.

Prayer *Lord, there are many decisions I make for my friends, family, church, and organization. Help me make them with your wisdom, having inquired of you. May I never justify my actions by blaming you as the cause.*

Discussion Questions

What are some excuses I make to justify my actions in regard to my marriage, friendships, work, and spiritual life? _____

_____

_____

_____

What are some excuses you have heard people make in the past about their actions while attributing them to God?

_____

_____

_____

THOUGHTS _____

_____

_____

_____

_____

_____

_____

Sometimes Pain Is the Payment for Good Work

Unfortunately, sometimes people repay your goodness with agony. Due to great insecurity in people's lives, sometimes doing what is right will result in pain.

1 Samuel 23:8: And Saul called up all his forces for battle, to go down to Keilah to besiege David and his men.

David did a lot of good work for Saul. When Saul was struggling with his emotional health, David's harp brought comfort. When a giant Philistine champion named Goliath was oppressing all of Israel, David was the only one brave enough to face and defeat him. David later brought such great success to Saul's rule, a chant was sung about David that enraged Saul: "Saul has killed his thousands and David his ten thousand."

Though Saul was the king, he could not accept that David's winning was also a win for his own kingship and the nation he was ruling. Saul became insecure. He felt he had to be the "star," and David's stardom propagated jealousy and insecurity. Some people are so insecure, especially those who feel they must be better than everyone else, that any measure of success by a person who is ranked below them is viewed as a threat.

Unfortunately, when those who are "above" feel threatened, their natural tendency is to respond by abusing their power to either make their subordinates extremely uncomfortable or completely try to eliminate them. Whether there are issues of race, gender, age, or political affiliations, human nature is very sensitive. This feeling of vulnerability is a product of shame that can be traced to the original sin by Adam and Eve.

There are times in our lives where our successes will make other people feel like a failure. If they have the means to strike against us, they will. A natural response to the stress of feeling threatened is to fight. Just as a bee will sting you if it perceives you as a threat or is frightened by your presence, people will respond in a similar fashion. This is not an excuse to do the wrong thing.

Throughout history, people have suffered great abuse because of other people's sins. When this happens to us, especially when it is caused by us doing right, we must respond with grace, truth, and love and allow God to avenge in His good time.

Prayer *Lord, there are times when doing the right thing will cause the ire of people to hurt me. Help me have the strength and courage to continue doing right despite the pain.*

 Discussion Questions

When have you done the right thing but received anguish instead of praise? _____

_____

_____

Why are so many of the world's great achievements accomplished through great suffering and injustice? _____

_____

_____

Are there times when you were wrong and did not understand the motives of another? _____

_____

_____

THOUGHTS _____

_____

_____

_____

_____

_____

The Desert of Preparation

Leaders must understand that when God allows you to be in a wilderness, the goal is not desolation but preparation.

1 Samuel 23:13-14, 24 "So David and his men, about six hundred in number, left Keilah and kept moving from place to place. . . . David stayed in the wilderness strongholds and in the hills of the Desert of Ziph. Day after day Saul searched for him, but God did not give David into his hands. . . . So, they set out and went to Ziph ahead of Saul. Now David and his men were in the Desert of Maon, in the Arabah south of Jeshimon."

There are times in life where it seems desolate, lonely, and hopeless. The Bible describes these places as the wilderness. It is a common tool God uses for the growth of his people. Before Israel could enter the Promised Land, he took them on a journey from Egypt to Israel in a span that is commonly referred to as forty years of wandering. The purpose was to root out all those who were unfaithful and filled with unbelief in order to raise up a new generation of Israelites who would be able to preserve the faith in preparation for Jesus to be born almost 1300 years after their entrance into Canaan.

Wilderness is often a period of waiting. Waiting for a spouse, waiting for a job, waiting for children, waiting for healing. The Biblical characters are no different. Abraham journeyed over a thousand miles from Ur to Canaan while waiting for a quarter-century for his promised son Isaac to be born. He would need to wait a total of 85 years until he could see his first grandchildren, Jacob and Esau.

Moses led Israel for forty years and was not able to enter the Promised Land, but before he would lead Israel at this crucial time, he spent forty years in the desert of Midian before the burning bush.

In this section, Saul is pursuing David. The future king must lead a band of six hundred from place to place in order to avoid Saul. A significant aspect of leadership is to guide your followers away from danger. Clearly, God's hand was on David. Whenever Saul would close in, God would prevent David from being delivered into Saul's hands. Saul was wasting valuable time and resources, pursuing the wrong goal.

One strategy David used to avoid Saul was to stay in wilderness strongholds and in the hills of the desert of Ziph. These would be difficult places for Saul to reach and allowed David a military advantage should Saul breakthrough and try to kill him. But because David needed to stay in these difficult places, living there would be a great challenge.

He and six hundred others would need to survive in a place of suffering and sparse resources. He is learning lessons on how to protect his military from harm, how to encourage his soldiers despite difficult circumstances, and how to organize people in order to survive. The most difficult circumstances David could experience would prove to be a training ground for him to learn how to shepherd the people of Israel (Psalm 78:72).

Prayer Lord, help me have peace and joy during my stay in the wilderness, knowing it is a time of growth, training, and preparation for your purposes to come.

 Discussion Questions

Think of a time where you felt like you were in a desert-like David. What did God teach you? _____

_____

_____

Why is the "waiting" part of being in the wilderness? _____

_____

_____

Think of a great leader you admire. Did they experience difficult circumstances? _____

_____

_____

How did they overcome them? _____

_____

_____

The Wilderness of Protection

Leaders will face enemies who are actively trying to destroy them but rest in God's protection because their efforts will be thwarted.

1 Samuel 23:14: 14 David stayed in the wilderness strongholds and in the hills of the Desert of Ziph. Day after day Saul searched for him, but God did not give David into his hands.

The famous manager of the New York Yankees and Mets, Casey Stengel, once said, "The key to being a good manager is keeping the five guys who hate you away from the four guys who have not made up their minds." Public speakers often refer to a rule that ten percent of the people who listen to them will not like them no matter how well they speak while another ten percent will like them no matter how bad they speak, but it is the eighty percent in the middle that need to be won.

The reality of leadership is that leaders will have opponents, and these enemies will often try to eliminate you. Many, like Saul, feel threatened. Whether it is someone in power over you who fears your prowess will cause the organization to take away the leader's job or someone below you who believes that their mission is to remove you from your position, enemies are present and seeking your demise. Some are easy to spot; they overtly dislike you and are naturally contentious. Others are harder to spot, feigning friendship while plotting your termination. Enemies are around. Almost everyone has one. Take heart. God is in control and will protect you.

Prayer Father, help me not fear my enemies. You will protect me.

 Discussion Questions

Think back to a time when you were in danger, but God protected you. What are the areas that cause fear in you?

_____

_____

How can faith in God assuage these fears? _____

_____

_____

THOUGHTS

_____

_____

_____

_____

_____

_____

Life-Strengthening Friendship

The demands and relationships of leaders are so great that there needs to be at least one relationship that strengthens you.

1 Samuel 23:16-18: "16 And Saul's son Jonathan went to David at Horesh and helped him find strength in God. 17 "Don't be afraid," he said. "My father Saul will not lay a hand on you. You will be king over Israel, and I will be second to you. Even my father Saul knows this." 18 The two of them made a covenant before the Lord. Then Jonathan went home, but David remained at Horesh."

Life includes relationships, and so does leadership. These relationships can be the difference between a life-giving occupation or a life-draining responsibility. From being a supervisor, employee, leaders of other organizations, to donors and friends, to be a leader means you will interact with many people.

One crucial relationship for a leader to have is, at the very least, one life-giving friend, someone who leaves you better off than when he or she came. This person should be a peer, someone who is close in position, the same gender, and one who understands who you are while not being threatened by you. David found that life-giving friend in Jonathan.

Jonathan would be a person who should be most threatened by David. As mentioned before, as the son of Saul, Jonathan would be the heir to the throne. But recognizing that David is the one

God has chosen, Jonathan orders his life to serve David instead of trying to kill him like his father. The Scriptures say that Jonathan strengthened David. David desperately needed this friendship and greatly mourned when he heard the news that Jonathan had died.

Leaders make countless relationships, and many of them drain life from the soul. Leaders must have at least one person whose presence brings strength to the heart.

Prayer — *Father, bring me a friend who can strengthen me as Jonathan did for David. If you have already given them to me, who are they, and how can I spend more time with them?*

 Discussion Questions

Outside of my spouse, who are my closest friends? _____

_____

_____

How do they give me life? _____

_____

_____

Where can I find friends who will breathe life into me?

_____

_____

When were these friends formed? _____

_____

_____

THOUGHTS _____

_____

_____

_____

_____

_____

The Apple of Awareness

*Spiritual leaders must develop a relentless awareness
of the presence of God in their life.*

1 Samuel 24:5-7: 5 Afterward, David was conscience-stricken for having cut off a corner of his robe.6 He said to his men, "The Lord forbid that I should do such a thing to my master, the Lord's anointed, or lay my hand on him; for he is the anointed of the Lord."7 With these words David sharply rebuked his men and did not allow them to attack Saul. And Saul left the cave and went his way.

Life means people. Some will become dear friends, others acquaintances, and then there will be those who become our enemies and want our demise. We cherish the first and disdain the later, but, for most of us, enemies will enter our lives. A full life is a life of love, but part of loving people is to love those who are our enemies (Matthew 5:43-48).

God puts people in our lives that are difficult to love. They range from the socially awkward, the homely looking, and the hurting, to people who misunderstand us or just do not like us for some specific reason. In the end, no dear friend can provide the inner peace that faith, hope, and love in an all-powerful, all fulfilling God can. This is what David had, a deep awareness of the presence of God, and it was this presence that allowed David to obey God and wait for his timing to remove the threat Saul posed to his very being.

One key to finding inner peace in life is to possess the "God-awareness" that David had. The burdens, pressures, and stress of life can tempt us to have an over fixation on ourselves. But a "God-awareness" David had helped us retain rationality and allows us to live our lives in a way that is pleasing to God.

David lived under extreme stress. Saul tried to kill him. Similarly, David experienced a minimum of two opportunities to kill Saul and take his rightful place as the next king of Israel, but David knew God would anoint him in his time. So, when opportunities presented themselves when David could kill Saul, David chose not to. David knew that as long as God allowed Saul to remain on the throne, David was to wait.

David was anointed king years before he would assume the throne. With this knowledge, David would be totally justified in taking Saul's life. But David chose not to and allowed God to remove Saul in his timing.

Are there enemies in your life? Are there people who desire your demise? Is there anyone who wants you fired? Anyone who wants you to suffer? Is there anyone who is threatened by you and has spread false rumors or created a false reality about you based on lies?

We cannot escape people, and some will be enemies and want your failure. Building "God-awareness," as David did, will prevent us from "killing the king" too early and produce in us a sense of peace and rationality that will allow us to obey God despite trying circumstances.

Prayer Father, please help me not focus on what I want or what I need but help me have my faith and hope in your goodness, sovereignty, and timing. There are many people who desire my demise or who would be happy if trouble fell on my life, help me not desire their punishment or elimination, but help me desire a blessing for them and to see the situation through your eyes and not my own.

Discussion Questions

Who are the people in my life who are difficult to love?

_____

_____

Are there people who would be happy if trouble fell on me? _

_____

_____

How is my thought life? _____

_____

_____

Do I view the world through what is best for me, or do I view the world through how I can bring God pleasure? _____

_____

_____

ENDNOTES

1 Taken from https://psychcentral.com/lib/what-is-emotional-intelligence-eq/ accessed April 27, 2017.

2 This section was aided by http://daveleingang.com/home/people-dont-follow-titles-they-follow-courage/ accessed May 10, 2017.

3 Taken from https://www.merriam-webster.com/dictionary/courage accessed May 10, 2017.

4 Both quotes taken from http://daveleingang.com/home/people-dont-follow-titles-they-follow-courage/ accessed May 10, 2017.

5 https://www.merriam-webster.com/dictionary/success accessed May 16, 2017.

6 Taken from: https://www.brainyquote.com/quotes/albert_einstein_143096 accessed December 19, 2017.

7 https://www.theguardian.com/commentisfree/2013/dec/06/desmond-tutu-nelson-mandela Accessed March 2, 2018.

8 S.D. Gordon, Quiet Talks on Prayer (New York, Chicago, Toronto, London, and Edinburgh: Fleming H. Revell Company, 1904), 233.

9 https://www.brainyquote.com/search_results?q=excuses

CPSIA information can be obtained
at www.ICGtesting.com
Printed in the USA
LVHW082135170821
695542LV00019B/456